# GREAT MARQUES
# JAGUAR

# GREAT MARQUES
# JAGUAR
## Chris Harvey

**Foreword by**
**Stirling Moss**
General Editor
**John Blunsden**

**First published in 1982 by
Octopus Books Limited,
59 Grosvenor Street,
London W1**

© 1982 Octopus Books Limited

ISBN 0 7064 1687 2

Produced by Mandarin Publishers Limited,
22a Westlands Road, Quarry Bay,
Hong Kong

Printed in Hong Kong

**Author's note**

It is always a pleasure to write about Jaguar – you get so much help from
the factory and the owners. One of the most enthusiastic is the man who
started it all, Sir William Lyons, who, with Alan Hodge and Clive
Richardson at the factory, Graig Hinton of Classic Cars of Coventry Ltd,
Nigel Dawes, Mike Cooper, Joss Davenport, David Harvey and Rick
Reading at the Jaguar Drivers' Club, gave so much help. These books are
made by their photographs, however, and I have to thank Ian Dawson for
the special photography.
Where possible, owners and custodians of the cars, at the time of
photography, are mentioned in the captions to the illustrations.

Chris Harvey

Special photography
**by Ian Dawson**

# Contents

*ENDPAPERS, PAGES 1–5 The D type Jaguar was one of the most beautiful cars ever made. This example, registered OKV 3, which gave the model its first success—at Rheims in 1954—is seen above being driven by Mike Hawthorn in the 1955 International Trophy sports car race at Silverstone (in which he finished fourth), and in the main picture by its current owner, Martin Morris.*

# Foreword by
# Stirling Moss

I was delighted to be asked to write a foreword for this book. I've driven scores of different makes of car during my racing years, and in the course of road-testing all the new production models for various magazines. Some of them can be hard to remember afterwards—but I'll always have fond memories of the Jaguars in my life. They've always had a richly deserved reputation for combining performance and comfort in a way which very few other makes could match. Normally, you couldn't have both—unless you had the good sense to see what Sir William Lyons and his team had to offer. And if you did, then you could have the best of both worlds at a price unmatched by any of their closest competitors. It was almost unfair!

Rather fewer people may also recall that Jaguar had a fairly short but still highly spectacular racing history. Not only were Jaguars a familiar sight, taking the chequered flag in all kinds of events from saloon-car races to the TT, but they made the Le Mans 24-hour race a Jaguar benefit for season after season, just as the Bentleys did in the 1920s, though in the Jaguar case they had to beat the might of Ferrari time after time to achieve that distinction.

Yet for me, the heart of the Jaguar magic is how close the two—racing car and road car—always were, beneath the bodywork, and in the solid virtues they shared. Rather than recalling any of the races I won driving Jaguars, my memory returns to an endurance test I took part in at Montlhéry in August 1952, when Leslie Johnson, Bert Hadley, Jack Fairman and I set out to drive an XK120 coupé for seven days and nights on end at 100 mph! Apart from a larger sump and a 24-gallon fuel tank, that car was virtually standard, and it stood up to the task magnificently. The only problems we had were due to the roughness of the track—before we started the run proper, a flake of loose concrete caused a blow-out on the banking, and eventually a rear spring had to be replaced, which put paid to any hope of an official 7-day record. Yet that apart, this standard production model went on and on, pounding round that banked track for seven days and seven nights—much of it in terrible weather—at an officially timed average of 100.31 mph, which collected no less than four world records and five class C international records. At the end of the run, it was driven back to London through ordinary everyday traffic, with no signs of stress or misbehaviour—no wonder people like me will always feel that the Jaguar is something special in the world of motor cars!

Now all successful car companies usually have a good story to tell—but the biggest problem with a company like Jaguar is that there's so much worth the telling that any writer has to steer a very narrow line between covering too much detail, and leaving out vital information. But I'm pleased to say this book has the mixture about right, with the racing story, the production cars and the experimental prototypes all given their fair share of attention. I can thoroughly recommend it—to dedicated Jaguar fans, and to newcomers to this splendid and fascinating story alike.

Stirling Moss
London

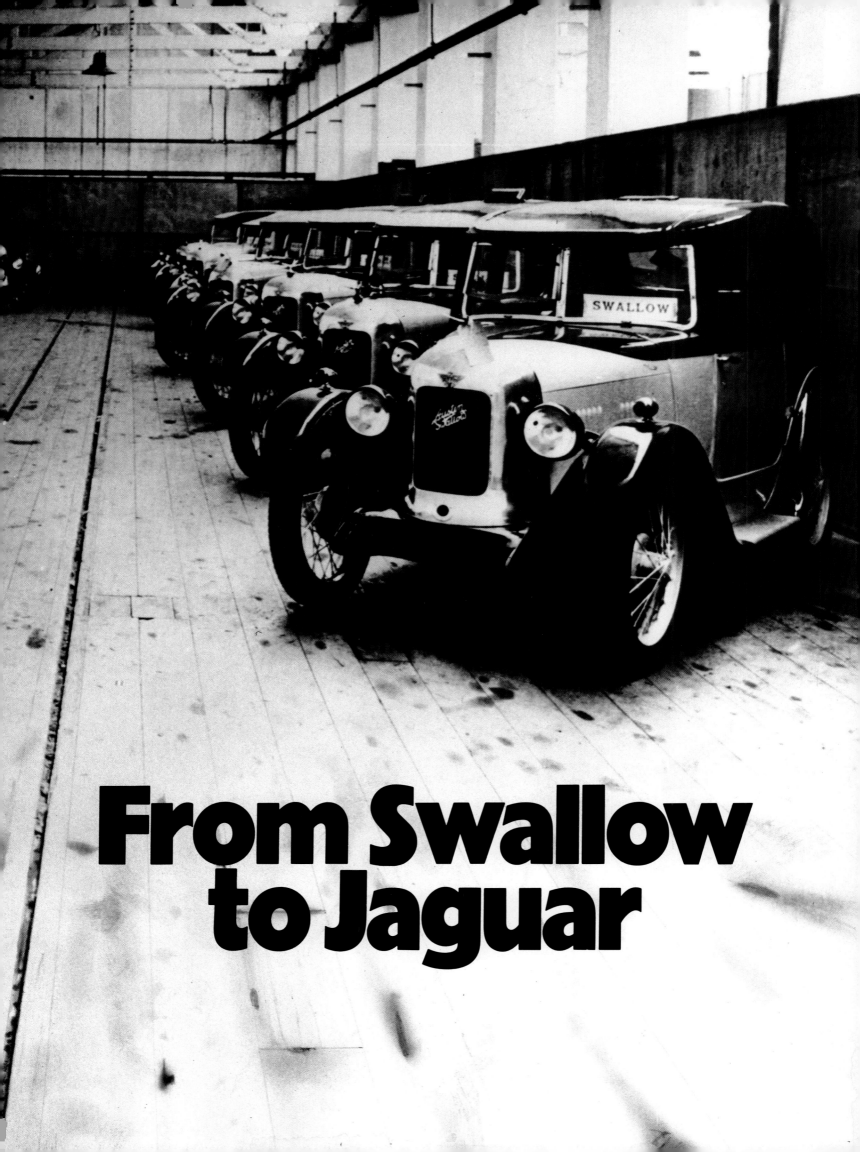

# From Swallow to Jaguar

The story of Jaguar concerns a company that started in a shed in 1920 and went on to produce the best car in the world; it centres on one man, an inspired stylist named William Lyons. His personality was stamped on everything the company made and in 1956 he received a knighthood for his services to the British motor industry. Although it was cars that brought lasting fame to the name Jaguar, the company's roots lay in motorcycle sidecars. These were products of the fertile imagination of William Walmsley, an English coal merchant's son who built his first sidecar at his family home in Stockport, Cheshire, in 1920. It was a wonderful-looking device, shaped like a cigar and unlike anything seen before. By 1921, his family had moved to the seaside resort of Blackpool in Lancashire, where Walmsley continued to make sidecars behind their new home. His activities quickly attracted the attention of a young neighbour, William Lyons. Although only 20 years of age, Lyons was determined to succeed in big business. Walmsley was not so concerned, but nevertheless they went into partnership to produce sidecars in quantity, backed by their respective fathers. They chose the name Swallow for their business, as Lyons was already firmly of the opinion that the name of animals and birds known for their speed and grace presented the ideal image.

Business expanded rapidly when the Swallow Sidecar Company was set up in 1922, although to keep down overheads Lyons made sure that it did so with a minimum of staff. Soon the partnership was occupying three separate workshops in Blackpool and was big enough to exhibit at the Motor Cycle Show at London's Olympia in 1923. This led to the establishment of a chain of Swallow dealers. At that time Walmsley and Lyons shared equal authority in the direction of the company although Lyons usually appeared in public as spokesman, mainly because of Walmsley's rather retiring nature. He was a brilliant stylist, however, and Lyons learned much from this man, ten years his senior. Between them they also showed exceptional ability at keeping down costs, not by skimping but by adopting efficient methods of using labour and material. Sidecar building tended to be a rather seasonal occupation, however, and by 1926 the rapidly expanding company was considering moving into car bodies, for which there was a demand all the year round. In addition, it was obvious even at that date that the car had more of a future than the motorcycle. With this in mind, the firm was renamed the Swallow Sidecar and Coachbuilding Company in 1926.

### The first Swallow car bodies
New, larger premises were acquired to bring the whole operation under one roof in Blackpool and more skilled workers taken on from factories in the English Midlands, which was already the centre of Britain's motor industry: labour was highly mobile in those days of rising unemployment. In January 1927, Lyons persuaded Stanley Parker, a dealer in Bolton, Lancashire, to supply him with a new Austin Seven chassis. So the first Swallow-bodied Austin was built, largely as a result of the efforts of Cyril Holland, a coachbuilder who had been hired from the Midlands. Several other manufacturers had tried their hands at supplying bodywork for Austin's popular small-car chassis, but the Swallow proved to be highly competitive. It cost less than larger vehicles with coachbuilt bodies, but was still a stylish luxury car. It met a demand when hard times were already hitting the people who had hitherto been able to afford special bodies, but did not yet want to be seen in a run-of-the-mill car.

Sidecar production built up to around 100 a week and continued through 15 distinct models until 1929 as car bodies began to occupy more of the partners' time. The Swallow's coachwork was distinctive in that aluminium panels were used rather than the fabric construction popular with many contemporary competitors, and it lasted longer as a result. The bodies were also usually finished in bright colours, such as crimson and cream, rather than the more commonly used black. A larger Morris Cowley-based Swallow was introduced soon after the Austin Swallow in 1927. Car bodies provided bigger profits for the emergent coachbuilders, but involved larger overheads; a lot of money was spent on transporting chassis up to Blackpool from their manufacturers in the Midlands and on subsequent storage of the bulkier products before distribution. There was also a chronic shortage of sufficiently skilled labour in Blackpool. This situation, together with a serious lack of space, led Lyons to search for a new, far larger factory in the Midlands.

*PREVIOUS PAGES Swallow-bodied Austin Sevens await delivery from Foleshill. The rails used to move munitions on trucks are clearly visible.*

*PREVIOUS PAGES. INSET An early Swallow sidecar in combination with a Rover motorcycle. Provided by Jaguar Cars Ltd.*

### The move to Foleshill and the first SS cars
Eventually an old ammunition factory was taken over at Foleshill, Coventry, and the firm moved lock, stock and barrel in 1928, taking many workers with it, and recruiting many more locally. Car bodies continued to be produced alongside sidecars, with a brief run of FIAT Swallows in 1929, before special coachwork was mounted on first Swift, and then Standard, chassis in 1930. As with the Austin production, which continued, Swallow was by now offering all types of body styles, particularly sporting two-seaters, the more luxurious drophead coupés, and saloons. Wolseley chassis also received Swallow bodies in 1931 before Lyons and Walmsley became car manufacturers in their own right with the SS1 of 1931.

The chassis of the new car was made by one of the existing suppliers, Standard, but it was available only for Swallows, so the resultant product was a distinctive car in its own right, rather than just a special body on a chassis shared with another company. Exactly what the initials SS stood for is still open to conjecture, but it is often assumed that they meant Standard Special. The first SS1 was a long, low, rakish fixed-head coupé with the option of six-cylinder engines of 2054 cc or 2552 cc. At the same time, a smaller, four-cylinder coupé was introduced with a 1006 cc engine, called the SS2; but it was the SS1 that captured everybody's imagination because of its outstanding styling and extraordinarily low price of just over £300. Lyons and Walmsley had achieved this by their well-known cost-cutting methods and by planning for a long production run to save tooling up for a new model every year, as so many other manufacturers did. Lyons's confidence in his product was justified by substantial sales, which kept the company in good profit.

### The founding of SS Cars Ltd
Demand for the new SS cars was such that production of the other Swallow-bodied cars was run down in 1932 and ceased in 1933 as the SS1 and SS2 ranges were increased to include tourers and, in 1934, saloons. At the same time, Lyons formed a new company called SS Cars Ltd to handle his burgeoning brainchild. However, other people did not feel so happy about SS cars. They sniped at them, saying they were not nearly as fast as they looked, although a couple of SS1 tourers had done well in the 1933 Alpine Trial. Lyons took such criticism to heart, and started a quest for more power to ensure his cars lived up to their appearance. Initially, larger engines, of 2143 cc and 2663 cc for the SS1 and 1343 cc and 1608 cc for the SS2, were fitted in 1934. Walmsley was not happy with the way things were going and resigned at the first annual general meeting

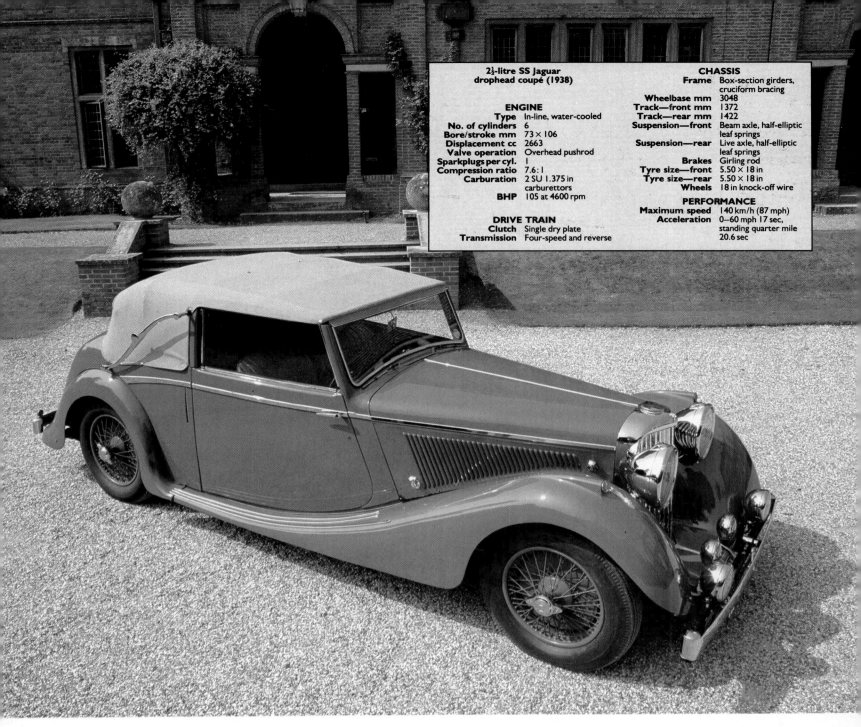

**2½-litre SS Jaguar
drophead coupé (1938)**

### ENGINE

| | |
|---|---|
| Type | In-line, water-cooled |
| No. of cylinders | 6 |
| Bore/stroke mm | 73 × 106 |
| Displacement cc | 2663 |
| Valve operation | Overhead pushrod |
| Sparkplugs per cyl. | 1 |
| Compression ratio | 7.6 : 1 |
| Carburation | 2 SU 1.375 in carburettors |
| BHP | 105 at 4600 rpm |

### DRIVE TRAIN

| | |
|---|---|
| Clutch | Single dry plate |
| Transmission | Four-speed and reverse |

### CHASSIS

| | |
|---|---|
| Frame | Box-section girders, cruciform bracing |
| Wheelbase mm | 3048 |
| Track—front mm | 1372 |
| Track—rear mm | 1422 |
| Suspension—front | Beam axle, half-elliptic leaf springs |
| Suspension—rear | Live axle, half-elliptic leaf springs |
| Brakes | Girling rod |
| Tyre size—front | 5.50 × 18 in |
| Tyre size—rear | 5.50 × 18 in |
| Wheels | 18 in knock-off wire |

### PERFORMANCE

| | |
|---|---|
| Maximum speed | 140 km/h (87 mph) |
| Acceleration | 0—60 mph 17 sec, standing quarter mile 20.6 sec |

*FAR LEFT The SS1 Airline saloon produced in 1936 was one of Sir William Lyons's most beautiful cars. Provided by British Leyland Heritage and Jaguar Cars Ltd.*

*ABOVE The 2½-litre SS Jaguar drophead coupé shown here was among the first all-steel bodied cars built at Foleshill. Provided by Joss Davenport and Mike Freeth.*

*LEFT A stripped-down track machine known as Old Number Eight was the fastest car built by SS before World War 2. It was subject to much development by works engineer Wally Hassan, who later helped design the XK engine and Coventry Climax Grand Prix power units before returning to Jaguar to work on the V12 used today. Old Number Eight was rebuilt in the late 1960s by David Barber to race again in the form shown.*

11

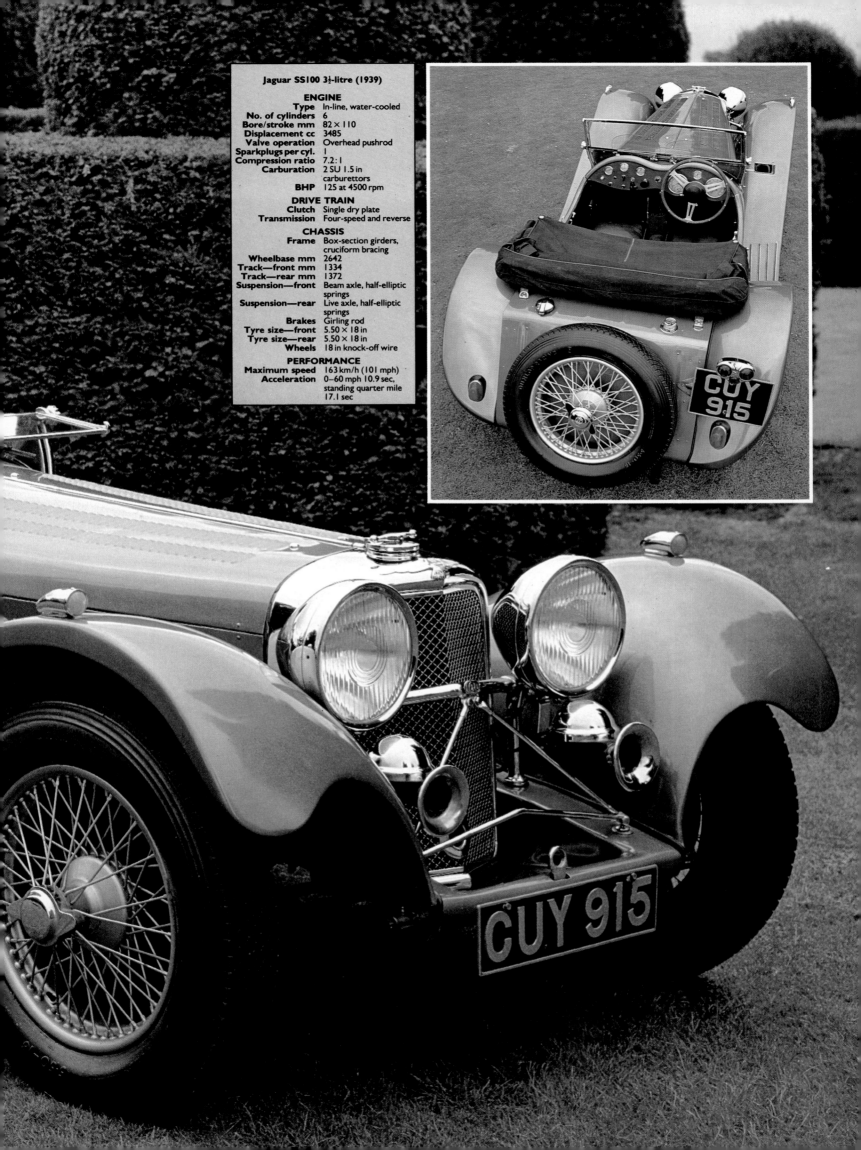

**Jaguar SS100 3½-litre (1939)**

### ENGINE
| | |
|---|---|
| Type | In-line, water-cooled |
| No. of cylinders | 6 |
| Bore/stroke mm | 82 × 110 |
| Displacement cc | 3485 |
| Valve operation | Overhead pushrod |
| Sparkplugs per cyl. | 1 |
| Compression ratio | 7.2 : 1 |
| Carburation | 2 SU 1.5 in carburettors |
| BHP | 125 at 4500 rpm |

### DRIVE TRAIN
| | |
|---|---|
| Clutch | Single dry plate |
| Transmission | Four-speed and reverse |

### CHASSIS
| | |
|---|---|
| Frame | Box-section girders, cruciform bracing |
| Wheelbase mm | 2642 |
| Track—front mm | 1334 |
| Track—rear mm | 1372 |
| Suspension—front | Beam axle, half-elliptic springs |
| Suspension—rear | Live axle, half-elliptic springs |
| Brakes | Girling rod |
| Tyre size—front | 5.50 × 18 in |
| Tyre size—rear | 5.50 × 18 in |
| Wheels | 18 in knock-off wire |

### PERFORMANCE
| | |
|---|---|
| Maximum speed | 163 km/h (101 mph) |
| Acceleration | 0–60 mph 10.9 sec, standing quarter mile 17.1 sec |

*ABOVE* The Mark V Jaguar was an interim model between the prewar SS and the car on which Sir William Lyons pinned many of his hopes of success after World War 2, the Mark VII saloon. Nevertheless, the 1950 Mark V was one of the most elegant Jaguars built. Provided by Classic Cars of Coventry, owner P.J. Masters.

*PREVIOUS PAGES* The SS 100 sports car was Sir William Lyons's most memorable prewar product, combining great beauty with an extremely good performance on road and track. The car illustrated here was one of the last produced in 1939. It has survived in fine condition with its original interior and colour. Provided by the Nigel Dawes Collection.

of SS Cars Ltd. He went on to pursue a low-key career in caravans and garage management, as Lyons nurtured his company by creating an engineering department in his search for better performance. At the same time a spectacular new Airline saloon was added to the SS range for 1935.

The first results of Lyons's bid to improve the performance of SS cars were seen in work performed on the 2.6-litre engine by the brilliant freelance gas-flow expert, Harry Weslake. The new unit was a great improvement on the old and it was used at first in a special lightweight two-seater version of the SS1, called the SS90 because it was good for 90 mph. This beautiful short-wheelbase vehicle was to be the forerunner of one of the most spectacular sports cars made before the Second

used the existing 1.6-litre unit from the SS2. The SS90 was to continue as the SS100 with the overhead-valve engine taking its performance past the 160 km/h (100 mph) mark. The SS1's touring body was fitted to the new saloon's chassis to cover that body option. Lyons intended the new range to last at least as long as the SS1 and SS2 and gambled on dramatically low prices to encourage volume sales: only £385 for the saloon, which even experts estimated to be worth twice as much! Such a new range also deserved a distinctive new name and, after consultation with advertising agents, Lyons decided on that of an animal renowned for its grace and speed: Jaguar.

The new SS Jaguars were a great success, even for a company that had become accustomed to rapidly expanding profits and turnover. SS100s also did well in competition, particularly a works-supported car registered BWK 77, driven by journalist Tommy Wisdom and magistrate Sammy Newsome. Frequently this car was stripped for track work and soon became known as Old Number Eight, after its chassis plate in the absence of number plates! The demand for the new SS Jaguars was so great that production methods at Foleshill had to be revised dramatically to meet orders. Lyons had little choice but to go over to all-steel bodywork in 1937 in place of the more traditional ash frame and steel panel system, which took longer to assemble. The teething troubles encountered while introducing this new method of construction were considerable and nearly bankrupted the company! But SS Cars survived the crisis thanks to the dedicated efforts of the company's workforce. The tourer was replaced by a drophead coupé based on the saloon and a new 3485 cc engine introduced as a further option. The performance with this unit, which produced 125 bhp, was exceptional, especially in the SS100 sports car. The small saloon received a revised 1.8-litre overhead valve engine.

By the end of 1938, production was running at the rate of more than 5000 cars a year and the time was ripe for further expansion. Brooklands race tuning ace Wally Hassan was taken on as chief experimental engineer under chief engineer Heynes, as Lyons started thinking about a new engine all of his own. Plans for that had to be shelved, however, as war intervened in 1939 and SS Cars went over to aircraft and prototype work. It was late in the war, during routine civil defence duties at the factory involving watching for fires, that Lyons, Heynes, Hassan and chief engine designer Claude Baily began dreaming up the new unit, of which more in the next chapter.

### The postwar export drive

When the war was over in 1945, the initials SS—which had been for ever tainted by their association with Hitler's élite Nazi corps—were dropped to be replaced by, simply, Jaguar. New staff were hired to supplement the original workforce who had survived the war; the most notable of the new appointments was F.R.W. 'Lofty' England, a former racing mechanic taken on as service manager in 1946. Before the war, SS Jaguars had sold well abroad, so Lyons managed to secure sufficient steel for a new export drive. In the early postwar years, steel in Britain was rationed and available only to those who could sell their products overseas. Lyons also managed to buy the Standard tooling to continue production of the 2.6-litre and 3.5-litre engines. The 1.8-litre engine was still available from Standard, so the postwar range was launched substantially as before, with three engine capacities, in saloon and drophead forms. The SS100 was dropped to avoid complication. Left-hand-drive versions of these cars, known retrospectively as the Jaguar Mark IVs, were introduced from August 1947 with a special eye on the United States. Although they cost nearly twice as much as their prewar equivalents, they were still very cheap by postwar standards, and sold well.

Meanwhile Heynes and company had been busy developing the new engine and an ingenious independent front suspension system to improve the car's ride and handling. The new engine was so revolutionary that it could not be put into volume production immediately, but was introduced in a sensational new sports car, the XK120, in 1948. The XK120 (see the next chapter) used a shortened version of a new chassis with the independent front suspension that was intended for a new saloon, the Mark VII, which is described later. (It was designated the Mark VII, rather than Mark VI, to avoid confusion with Bentley's rival Mark Six.) Such was the complexity of the body for the Mark VII that it could not be put into production until 1950, and in the meantime its chassis was used on an interim model, the Mark V, which replaced the Mark IV Jaguars in 1948. The Mark V was available only with the old 2.6-litre and 3.5-litre engines, and used bodywork developed from the Mark IVs. Like all the other Jaguars before, it sold successfully, but the world was waiting for the new Jaguars.

World War. No sooner had the SS90 been introduced in March 1935 than a gifted young engineer, William Heynes, was lured from Humber to coordinate the new engineering department: a vital step in Lyons's plan to become self-sufficient and not dependent on others for his mechanical components.

### The first Jaguars

One of Heynes's first tasks was to help revise the by now complex SS range for 1936: its most important car was to be a new four-door saloon powered by a Weslake overhead-valve conversion on the 2.6-litre engine, which boosted its output from 70 bhp to 105! A smaller version

# The excellent XKs

The XK120 that was unveiled at the London Motor Show in 1948 was the sports car that had everything: a roadster body more beautiful than anything even Jaguar had produced before; an immensely strong chassis that had taken years to develop; and an engine so sophisticated that it looked as though it should have graced a Grand Prix racer rather than a sports car costing only £998! This was not only the first pure-bred Jaguar engine, it was also the world's first mass-production engine with twin overhead camshafts and hemispherical combustion chambers. Such technical sophistication had only been seen before in racing cars costing a great deal of money and produced only in very small quantities. Lyons, who was the inspiration behind the engine, gambled once more on its staying in production for so long that the tooling and development costs would amount to only a tiny sum on each engine. But even he could not have guessed that the XK unit would be so successful that it would still be powering Jaguars into the 1980s!

## The genesis of the XK engine

When this unit was still in the design stage during the war-time fire-watching sessions, even engineers as experienced and adventurous as Heynes, Hassan, Baily and Harry Mundy doubted whether it would be possible to produce a twin overhead camshaft engine for a passenger car. They recognized the advantages of such a layout in that it produced tremendous power, but pointed out that it carried penalties: these engines tended to be very noisy because long chains or trains of gears were needed to drive the camshafts; they were difficult to make, which inevitably meant that they cost more, and were potentially less reliable; and they were far from easy to service. But Lyons would not settle for second best and insisted that he must have a 'twin cam'; what is more, it also had to look good! Once they had expressed their reservations, Heynes, Hassan, Baily and Mundy worked with a will that resulted in the sensational six-cylinder in-line XK unit that produced no less than 160 bhp from 3442 cc. They had the assistance of Harry Weslake, who was to help extract even more power from the engine as time went on. With bores of 83 mm, the XK engine had a relatively long stroke of 106 mm, which gave it impressive torque. Its crankshaft ran in seven main bearings; this

meant that the bottom of the engine was extremely strong, which it had to be to transmit the power produced by the top end. The cylinder block was cast in iron by Leyland Motors—the British truck firm that would much later figure prominently in Jaguar history—and the head made from alloy, which saved weight and dispersed heat more efficiently. At first the engine was produced in a relatively mild form of tune because it was feared that, had a more radical stage of tune been adopted by using higher-lift cams, inexperienced mechanics might damage the vital valve gear during the decarbonization process, so common in those days. However, the quality of fuel improved and 'decoking' became a relative rarity, and it was found that the average mechanic was so proud to work on such a magnificent engine that he did not 'mess it up'. In any case, the XK engine's 160 bhp was enough to propel the 1320 kg (2912 lb) car at more than 190 km/h (120 mph), hence the designation XK120.

A rather 'graunchy', but very reliable Moss four-speed manual gearbox was used in a shortened version of the Mark V saloon's ladder-design chassis. This used conventional half-elliptic leaf-spring rear suspension with a live axle, and Heynes's new independent front suspension, which employed wishbones and torsion bars parallel to the chassis sides. A feature of this front suspension was the brilliantly simple ball joints used to locate the stub axle carriers. Steering was a recirculating-ball type and so arranged that it could be set on either the right- or the left-hand side to cater for export markets from the start.

## The XK120 in production

At first the XK120 had an aluminium two-seater roadster body, built in the old manner on an ash frame because Lyons did not envisage making many of these cars. He saw them principally as a mobile test bed for the engine and an advertisement for his planned Mark VII saloon, which would use the same unit in the longer Mark V chassis. The great expense of assembling the giant presses and tools needed for all-steel body construction could be justified only if a large number of cars was to be produced. As it happened, there was such a demand for the car that he had to do just that, although it took until 1950 to tool up for the first all-steel XK120. The demand had been set off, first, by the car's spectacular

ABOVE *The XK120 super sports model was the car that took the motoring world by storm in the late 1940s and early 1950s, combining exceptional elegance with a fantastic performance. Provided by Joss Davenport.*

PREVIOUS PAGES *One of the most successful competition Jaguars was the XK120 rally car driven by Ian and Pat Appleyard. It can be seen at Britain's National Motor Museum. Provided by British Leyland Heritage and Jaguar Cars Ltd.*

| Jaguar XK120 super sports (1951) | | CHASSIS | |
|---|---|---|---|
| **ENGINE** | | Frame | Box-section girders, cruciform bracing |
| Type | In-line, water-cooled | Wheelbase mm | 2591 |
| No. of cylinders | 6 | Track—front mm | 1295 |
| Bore/stroke mm | 83 × 106 | Track—rear mm | 1270 |
| Displacement cc | 3442 | Suspension—front | Independent wishbone and torsion bar |
| Valve operation | Twin overhead camshafts | Suspension—rear | Live axle, half-elliptic springs |
| Sparkplugs per cyl. | I | Brakes | Lockheed hydraulic drums |
| Compression ratio | 8:1 (7:1 or 9:1 optional) | Tyre size—front | 6.00 × 16 in |
| Carburation | 2 SU 1.75 in carburettors | Tyre size—rear | 6.00 × 16 in |
| | | Wheels | 16 in wire or solid |
| BHP | 160 at 5000 rpm (180 at 5300 with special equipment) | **PERFORMANCE** (160 bhp model) | |
| | | Maximum speed | 201 km/h (125 mph) |
| **DRIVE TRAIN** | | Acceleration | 0–60 mph 10 sec, standing quarter mile 17 sec |
| Clutch | Single dry plate | | |
| Transmission | Four-speed and reverse | | |

RIGHT *Some of Jaguar's works XK120s have survived, notably one registered JWK 977. It is seen here (inset) with its original driver, Peter Walker, leading eventual winner, Stirling Moss, during the 1951 Silverstone Production Car Race, and 30 years later back at Silverstone for a historic race. The car has an interesting history, Jaguar having sold it to Hugh Howorth, who fitted C type rear suspension and won numerous races. Today, this famous XK120 is owned by John Foster.*

appearance and incredibly low price—there is some evidence that Lyons initially saw it as a loss leader—and, secondly, by a demonstration for the doubting Thomases that it really was capable of the performance claimed when test driver 'Soapy' Sutton managed 213.4 km/h (132.6 mph) with a mildly modified version before astonished journalists on the Jabbeke motorway in Belgium in May 1949. Only a V12 Ferrari costing four times as much and available only to selected racing teams could match this. So Jaguar, who had planned to spend the year making Mark Vs and preparing for production of the Mark VII, found itself with a bulging order book for XK120s.

**Competition successes for the XK120**

The first customer cars—mostly for export—left Foleshill in July 1949, a month before three were entered in the new Silverstone Production Car Race. It was Britain's first big motor race since the war in which production

cars could be compared, and two of the XKs, driven by Leslie Johnson and Peter Walker, left the field standing. Johnson, who won at Silverstone, went on to perform impressively in America before receiving a new works-supported XK120 in company with Walker, Wisdom, veteran Italian racing driver Clemente Biondetti, and rallyman Ian Appleyard, whose successes with an SS100 included a Coupe des Alpes in the Alpine Rally. Appleyard had special connections with the factory because, apart from being a Jaguar dealer, his crew consisted of his wife, Pat, who happened to be Lyons's daughter! And their car, registered NUB120, was to become one of the most successful competition Jaguars.

Johnson spearheaded Jaguar's assault on the classic Le Mans 24-hour race in 1950 and took his near-standard car up to third place, leaving many outright racing sports cars trailing, until failing brakes led to an overstrained clutch and eventual retirement. Many similar cars suffered from brake trouble in those days because of the development of all-

the retirement of Johnson's XK120 in the all-important Le Mans race, enthusiasts everywhere were extremely impressed by its showing against far more specialized machinery that could not be bought by ordinary people. And Heynes was convinced that, with a special competition version of the XK120, it would be possible to win at Le Mans. Lyons agreed and authorized the building of the C (for Competition) type, which went on in 1951 to the first of Jaguar's five victories at Le Mans, and is described in the 'Glory Years' chapter.

Meanwhile XK120s continued to win races all over the world and make up most of the fields in international rallies. By far the most successful XK120 rally drivers were the Appleyards with NUB 120, which they used to win the Alpine Rally (1950, 1951, 1952) and the Tulip Rally (1951) and many others in a life that extended to more than 100,000 miles!

In America, world champion-to-be Phil Hill bored out an XK120's cylinder block to 3.8 litres (which was to become a significant capacity in Jaguar history) and won numerous events; in Britain, the greatest driver never to win a world championship, Stirling Moss, made his name in the big time with one of the semi-works XK120s. Moss was offered the car in 1950 when Wisdom opted for an official works drive in a Jowett Jupiter in Britain's premier road race, the Tourist Trophy, held on Ulster's Dundrod circuit. Moss overtook Johnson to win in atrocious conditions and so impressed Lyons that he was signed to drive for Jaguar when the company ran a full works team of C types the following year. It was an excellent birthday present for Moss: he was to be 21 next day! He also made mincemeat of the opposition with an XK120 in the 1951 Silverstone Production Car Race.

Other drivers enjoyed notable success with XK120s, particularly the Belgians Jacques Ickx (whose son became a Grand Prix star) and Johnny Claes who won the 1951 Liège-Rome-Liège rally—in reality the world's roughest road race; former Spitfire pilot Duncan Hamilton; and Sir James Scott-Douglas, who helped start the glorious Scottish team, the Ecurie Ecosse.

### The XK120 fixed-head coupé

As these stalwarts raced on their alloy-bodied XK120s, steel-bodied cars, which weighed about 25 kg (56 lb) more, but looked almost exactly the same, had been in production since April 1950. Production of the Mark VII saloon finally started in October 1950, leaving Jaguar's staff free to work on a fixed-head version of the XK120, which was introduced in March 1951. It met the demand for a car as civilized as the Mark VII saloon without sacrificing the performance of the sports car. This new coupé was like an XK120 roadster (to use the American description which has now become universal; Jaguar preferred to call it a super sports) with an attractive steel top, the lines of which bore a close resemblance to those of the Mark VII. Wind-up windows replaced the roadster's sidescreens, the doors were fitted with exterior handles and the interior upholstered like the saloon, rather than the far more spartan—but lighter—roadster. Ventilation had received special attention, with quarter lights front and rear, following complaints about too much heat in the cockpit from people using the cars in hot climates. A heater was also fitted as standard following complaints from people living in cold climates about too little heat in the cockpit! Wire wheels—like those used on an increasing number of competition XK120s to assist brake cooling and fast wheel changing—were offered as a option. When these wheels were fitted to either the roadster or the fixed-head coupé, the rear spats had to be left off because of the protruding knock-off hub spinners.

Soon after, Jaguar provided more options in the form of tuning equipment for customers who wanted to use their XK120s (and Mark VIIs) in competition. These consisted chiefly of higher-lift camshafts, higher compression pistons, larger carburettors, stiffer springs and thicker brake pads; they were based on well-tried items used on the C type. These modifications could boost the engine's power to 190 bhp.

Demand for the XK120 and the Mark VII was so great that Jaguar was again faced with the old problem: the factory was not big enough. So Lyons started searching for new premises once more and managed to acquire a modern factory used by Daimler to make cars and buses. Daimler had made armoured cars there during the war, but its needs were contracting and in 1951 the firm decided to centralize its operation on the main works at Radford, Coventry. Jaguar was happy to move into the million square feet at Browns Lane, Allesley, on the outskirts of Coventry, which is still the company's home.

Meanwhile, the fixed-head coupé, which was not normally used in top-line racing because it was heavier than the roadster—although it found favour in winter rallies—was publicized in 1952 by a run at the Montlhéry

*ABOVE This is the car that Stirling Moss remembered so well, the bronze XK120 fixed-head coupé with which he broke nine international records at Montlhéry in 1952. It is just as his team left it, complete with two-way radio. Provided by British Leyland Heritage and Jaguar Cars Ltd.*

enveloping coachwork. These bodies, which were better streamlined than the old-fashioned types used on models such as the SS100, meant that cars were capable of higher speeds. The result was that the drum brakes suffered badly at the limit of their performance, as they had to stop the cars from far higher speeds and, because of the better streamlining, without the benefit of such a good flow of cooling air. This problem was made worse by a reduction in wheel sizes to take modern tyres, which meant that brake drums of smaller diameter had to be used to fit inside the wheels. It was a problem that was not really solved until the introduction of disc brakes, pioneered on competition Jaguars. Despite

track near Paris during which Johnson, Moss, Jack Fairman and Bert Hadley averaged 161.43 km/h (100.31 mph) for seven days and nights to cover 27,119 kilometres (16,851 miles) and take nine international records.

## The XK120 drophead coupé

The company was still recovering from the move to Browns Lane and it was not until April 1953 that a new Jaguar was launched—in this case a drophead coupé version of the XK120. This was more like the fixed-head car than the roadster, with a well-tailored folding hood replacing the steel roof. The roadster retained its spartan trim and the V-shaped windscreen that protected its occupants so well from the elements, whether the skimpy lightweight hood was up or stowed away: it was considered normal in those days to drive a roadster with the hood off in almost any weather.

The drophead coupé, however, was intended to be driven with the hood down only when the weather was really good. This was particularly important because the flatter, fixed-head style windscreen needed with the wind-up windows set up air currents that whipped around the back of the occupants' necks: fine on a good day but not so pleasant on a bad one!

## The XK140

Jaguar's engineers then devoted their energies to developing the legendary D type sports-racing car for Le Mans (see later) before revising the XK120 in the light of comments from sales forces, particularly in the export markets, which took most of the production. The result was the XK140, which used the same body pressings as the XK120 and was available in roadster, fixed-head and drophead forms, but was considerably different under the skin. The chassis was almost exactly the same as that of the XK120 except that the engine was moved forward 76 mm (3 in) to make more room in the cockpit and improve weight distribution from 48 per cent front and 52 per cent rear to nearer 50/50. The central crossmember was modified to allow an overdrive made by Laycock to be fitted as an option, the battery and bulkhead positions were changed, and rack and pinion steering was fitted. The rack, which had been developed for the C type, transformed the car in conjunction with the revised weight distribution and more up-to-date shock absorbers.

On the roadster and drophead cars the bulkhead was moved forward 76 mm (3 in) to give more room in the cockpit; on the fixed-head coupé the bulkhead was reshaped to give a similar effect without changing the roof pressing, although the roofline was raised 25 mm (1 in) to heighten the impression of airiness in the cockpit. The extra space liberated in the drophead (which also had a 25 mm—1 in—higher hood) and fixed-head

coupés was used for two tiny rear seats, which made the cars more appealing to families with small children. At a pinch, an adult could squeeze in the back across the seats for short journeys.

The XK140, which was introduced in October 1954, was easily identified because it had similar bumpers (fenders) to the Mark VII saloon, a development that gave better protection against clumsy parkers, and a different radiator grille with a new cooling system, following complaints about overheating in traffic. It was also a better car mechanically. The special-equipment XK120's engine was used as standard on all XK140s, with a single exhaust to give 180 bhp, or with a high-compression C type head and twin exhausts to give 210 bhp. The standard XK140 was called the XK140M in the United States (because of its 'modified' engine) and the XK140 with a C type head, the XK140MC, following similar, but unofficial, designations given to export XK120s. A close-ratio gearbox, which had been available as an option on XK120s since 1953, was now standardized, and more cars left the factory with wire wheels.

This range continued virtually unchanged until October 1956 as the factory concentrated on introducing the Mark 1 saloon (described in the chapter 'The Businessman's Express') and revising the Mark VII. It was at this point that automatic transmission like that offered on the Mark VII became available as an option on the drophead and fixed-head coupés.

## The XK150

Soon after, in May 1957, the XK was revised dramatically for the last time, as the XK150. The XK150, introduced at first in drophead and fixed-head forms, was as near as you could get to an XK saloon. It was bigger and heavier, but a good deal faster in the middle range of its performance because it was fitted with a new B type cylinder head. This developed only 190 bhp but gave the engine a lot more torque in mid-range. The C type head was still available for ultimate top-end performance and the original head became known as the A type. Almost as soon as the XK150 went into production, following considerable difficulties with a factory fire, it was fitted with disc brakes all round which—like the C type on which they had been pioneered—made the new car far faster from point to point.

The chassis and running gear of the XK150 were substantially the same as on the XK140, but the coachwork looked very different. The body was given a raised waistline with bulbous doors and wings to allow the interior to be widened by 102 mm (4 in). This gave the passengers more room; and they also benefited from a further raising of the scuttle line. A wrap-around windscreen was fitted now that glass of the right quality was available and the fixed-head coupé was given a large saloon-style rear window to make it feel more spacious and airy. Other body changes

LEFT During the 1950s the Scottish national team, the Ecurie Ecosse, brought glory to Britain racing Jaguars. It started with XK120s, one of which has survived: the car driven by Sir James Scott-Douglas. Provided by Tony Hildebrand of Straight Six.

RIGHT The XK140 was an XK120 updated to meet the demands of its largest market, America. As a result it had stronger bumpers and more room inside. Its steering was also improved, particularly to please the Europeans. This 1955 drophead coupé was provided by Alan Holdaway.

*ABOVE AND RIGHT The ultimate XK was the 150S model with the 3.8-litre engine produced in 1959 and 1960. This fixed-head coupé was capable of more than 210 km/h (130 mph), thanks to its triple-carburettor engine with straight-port cylinder head giving 265 bhp. It has all the extras, including sunroof and luggage rack. Provided by John Blake.*

included wrapping the rear bumper around the flanks for greater protection and fitting a wider radiator grille to improve cooling further. The fixed-head and drophead coupés shared a similar interior, but the XK150 roadster was far more spartan. This variant was not introduced until March 1958 because the factory was still recovering from the fire, and to have launched it earlier would have added complications to already stretched resources. Naturally this was a faster car because it was lighter, and it became even quicker when it was fitted with an optional straight-port cylinder head and triple carburettors, which increased the power to 250 bhp. In this form it was known as the XK150S. The brakes were improved at the same time by fitting square quick-change pads developed on the D type, in place of the older round type. At this point, wire wheels were fitted as standard on the special-equipment models and overdrive on the XK150S, which was not available with the option of an automatic gearbox: this was because it was intended primarily as a competition car. The S type options were made available on the fixed-head coupé from February 1959, but not on the drophead at first because it was intended purely as a touring car.

## The 3.8-litre XKs

Then, in October 1959, an enlarged engine was offered to provide even more power and torque. This was the 3.8-litre unit, which became available on all XK models; it had been under development by the factory since it was first used on a D type in 1956. The factory's version of the 3.8-litre XK unit was considerably different to what had been achieved by people such as Phil Hill. Jaguar stepped up the capacity of the factory engine to 3781 cc by increasing the bore to 87 mm in a new block with dry liners, rather than by boring out the existing 3.4-litre block, which had proved risky.

In this form, with a gold-painted 9:1 compression ratio straight-port cylinder head and triple SU carburettors, the XK150S 3.8-litre, as it was called, produced 265 bhp; with a blue-painted B type 9:1 compression head and twin SUs, it turned out 220 bhp with drops of about 10 bhp each for the 8:1 and 7:1 versions of this head. The lower compression ratios were normally used in export markets where only poor quality fuel was available. These cylinder head and carburettor options were also available on the 3.4-litre range, which was retained, giving a seemingly endless variety of power units. In these forms the Jaguar XK sports cars continued in production until the end of 1960, when they were discontinued to make way for the sensational new E type described later.

### Jaguar XK150S
### fixed-head coupé (1960)

**ENGINE**

| | |
|---|---|
| Type | In-line, water-cooled |
| No. of cylinders | 6 |
| Bore/stroke mm | 87 × 106 |
| Displacement cc | 3781 |
| Valve operation | Twin overhead camshafts |
| Sparkplugs per cyl. | I |
| Compression ratio | 9 : I |
| Carburation | 3 SU 2 in carburettors |
| BHP | 265 at 5500 rpm |

**DRIVE TRAIN**

| | |
|---|---|
| Clutch | Single dry plate |
| Transmission | Four-speed and reverse |

**CHASSIS**

| | |
|---|---|
| Frame | Box-section girders, cruciform bracing |
| Wheelbase mm | 2591 |
| Track—front mm | 1302 |
| Track—rear mm | 1302 |
| Suspension—front | Independent wishbone and torsion bar |
| Suspension—rear | Live axle, half-elliptic springs |
| Brakes | Dunlop disc all round |
| Tyre size—front | 6.00 × 16 in |
| Tyre size—rear | 6.00 × 16 in |
| Wheels | 16 in wire or solid |

**PERFORMANCE**

| | |
|---|---|
| Maximum speed | 212 km/h (132 mph) |
| Acceleration | 0–60 mph 7.8 sec, standing quarter mile 16.2 sec |

# Grace, Space and Pace

The Mark VII saloon introduced in 1950 laid the foundations of continuing prosperity for the Jaguar Car Company. It was the culmination of years of development and designed to sell in larger quantities than the XK sports car: although the XK achieved far greater popularity than anticipated, the saloon was still produced at the rate of about 100 per week against the XK's 60 or so. The reasons for its success were threefold: it was extremely good looking, it could carry up to six passengers in great comfort, and it was very fast. In fact, the advertising men who launched the Mark VII had no trouble in backing up their claim that it had unparalleled 'Grace, Space and Pace'.

William Lyons was at his most inspired when he designed the Mark VII's coachwork. It was a large car with voluptuous lines, but his talent for proportion made it also look graceful, even lithe. He did it all by eye, describing what he wanted to a team of craftsmen, who then built mock-ups in wood and metal as they used to do with sidecars. Lyons would cast his critical gaze on their efforts and ask for changes here and there until he was satisfied with the final product. Only then, in the case of the steel-bodied cars such as the Mark VII, did the draughtsmen make drawings for the giant tools to stamp out the body panels. Tooling for such big panels as the Mark VII needed took a long time to produce, which was one of the reasons for the delay in its production.

The chassis was the same as the Mark V saloon except that the 3.4-litre XK engine, which replaced the pushrod unit, was mounted 127 mm (5 in) further forward, to give more room in the passenger compartment. Three of these additional inches were used to increase the legroom at the back, and the other two inches were taken up by moving the rear seat forward. This meant that the rear wheel arches hardly intruded into the rear-seat space and the luggage boot (trunk) became very large. The rear-seat passengers also benefited enormously from an extra 127 mm (5 in) of interior space achieved by adopting full-width coachwork. This extra space contributed to the additional boot capacity, of course—an important factor in the American market. The Mark VII's 3048 mm (10 ft) wheelbase was no longer than that of most American cars, but its width—1854 mm (6 ft 1 in)—was greater and there was far less overhanging weight, ensuring better handling. This was vital because of the exceptional performance: with a maximum speed of 166 km/h (103 mph) and a 0–60 mph acceleration time of 13.4 seconds (acceleration standards were conventionally expressed in mph), it was in a class of its own.

Mechanically, the Mark VII was similar to the XK120 except that it had wider ratio gears, although the sports car's gearbox could be substituted for competition. Its finish and interior were to the highest standards, which made it even more exceptional value. The Bentley Continental, which was one of the few cars that could stay with a Mark VII, cost more than five times as much.

## Mark VII successes

This magnificent new saloon received a rapturous welcome when it was unveiled at the London Motor Show and revealed to the American public soon after in New York later in 1950. It sold well on appearance and a performance that had been confirmed by the exploits of the XK120, but sales received a further boost when two Mark VIIs, driven by Frenchmen René Cotton and Jean Heurteaux, finished fourth and sixth in the Monte Carlo Rally early in 1952. An Allard driven by its constructor, Sydney Allard, won, but his tiny South London firm could never produce enough cars to present a serious challenge to Jaguar in either the saloon car or sports car stakes. The heavy—1727 kg (3808 lb)—Mark VII had such good torque that it could plough through the deep snow drifts frequently encountered during this rally, which was the most important in the international calendar at the time.

By 1952, numerous races were being organized for sports cars, and it was decided to make the Silverstone Production Car Race open only to saloons so that it could retain its unique character as a showcase for cars that the man in the street could buy. Jaguar celebrated by mopping up the event yet again with a Mark VII driven by Stirling Moss! Ken Wharton was second in a Ford Zephyr, with Sydney Allard third in one of his saloons.

*PREVIOUS PAGES The Jaguar Mark VIII of 1957 enjoyed only a short production run before it was replaced by the Mark IX. This particular car was originally owned by a Norwegian Consul in Great Britain, and has a manual gearbox with overdrive. Provided by Graig Hinton of Classic Cars of Coventry Ltd.*

*RIGHT The Jaguar Mark VIIM used a more powerful version of the XK engine than the earlier Mark VII, to give a better performance which, when combined with other improvements, made a substantially updated and more attractive model for the 1955 season. This example also has a manual gearbox with overdrive and was provided by Graig Hinton of Classic Cars of Coventry Ltd.*

*BELOW One of the most extraordinary saloons built by Jaguar was a Mark VII designed for the Silverstone Production Car Race in 1954. It used the chassis of Sir William Lyons's personal car built in 1951, with a brand-new magnesium body to save weight. However, more standard models proved fast enough to win the race, so this lightweight was kept as a development hack. Eventually Jaguar publicist Bob Berry bought the car, fitted it with a D type engine, modified the suspension and terrorized saloon car races in the late 1950s! After six years as a runabout, it was sold to Doctor Christopher Sturridge, who lovingly restored it and still owns the car today.*

The Appleyards, who normally drove their XK120 in rallies, preferred a Mark VII for the Monte Carlo Rally, and came within a second of winning in 1953. They were beaten only by the very experienced Dutchman, Maurice Gatsonides, in a Ford Zephyr, with Irishman Cecil Vard—who came third in 1951—fifth in his much-travelled Mark V saloon. In 1953 Moss won the Silverstone Production Car Race again in a works Mark VII, and with Jaguar's second win at Le Mans in a C type, the Coventry firm's reputation was soaring. Sales certainly reflected Jaguar successes in racing and rallies!

**Automatic transmission and overdrive for the Mark VII**
Those customers who were more interested in labour-saving devices than outright sporting performance were not neglected either. By 1953, most Americans expected luxury cars to be available with automatic transmission. Rolls-Royce and Bentley were already offering this as an option, so Jaguar could not stand aloof. It would have cost the company much time and money to develop its own automatic gearbox, so Jaguar simply adapted a Borg-Warner, which had originated in America. The Borg-Warner box was modified slightly to suit the XK engine and fitted as an option to Mark VIIs from mid-1953. Then overdrive was offered as an extra on manual-gearbox cars from January 1954. This immediately became popular as a fuel-saving device in Europe, where pump prices were high, whereas the automatic gearbox was favoured in North America.

Meanwhile, the Mark VII went from strength to strength in the 1954 Monte Carlo Rally, with another Irishman, Ronnie Adams, beaten by just a few seconds by Grand Prix ace Louis Chiron in a Lancia Aurelia GT. Three of these massive saloons, driven by Appleyard, Le Mans winner Tony Rolt and Moss, then finished first, second and third in the 1954

Silverstone Production Car Race, despite a tough challenge from a team of Daimler Conquests.

**The Mark VIIM**
The Mark VII's performance was further improved with the introduction of the Mark VIIM in September 1954, which used a 190 bhp version of the 3.4-litre XK engine with a closer-ratio gearbox. Various styling changes were also made in keeping with those on the new XK140 sports car. A lightweight version of the old model, fitted with a 210 bhp XK engine, won the Silverstone Production Car Race yet again in 1955, driven by Mike Hawthorn, with the similar cars of Ian Stewart and Desmond Titterington second and third. The Mark VIIs won the team award in the Monte Carlo Rally that year with Adams in 8th place, Vard 27th, and R.D. Mattock 38th. It was during this year that the automatic transmission option was finally made available in Britain, before most of the large saloons were fitted with automatic gearboxes from 1956. This was because, by then, Jaguar had introduced a 2.4-litre compact saloon for the more sporting driver. These new cars, the Mark 1 and the Mark 2, are covered in the chapter 'The Businessman's Express'.

Despite the introduction of the much lighter Mark 1, the Mark VII was still successful in competition because of its larger, more powerful engine. By 1956, Jaguars had won most of the events worth entering, but the Monte Carlo Rally had eluded them. Adams came to the rescue with a tremendous drive in the 1956 event, which he won in company with Frank Biggar and Derek Johnston. His works Mark VIIM was the only car of more than 2500 cc to finish in the first 38 places, such was the weight of handicaps against big machines. It was a glorious swansong in competition for these Jaguars, which were as impressive as the *Queen Mary* or *Queen Elizabeth* ocean liners as they sailed along majestically.

29

## The Mark VIII and IX

These cars were constantly being improved in production, as the compact Jaguar saloons took over in competition. The B type cylinder head was fitted, the automatic gearbox further improved, and there was a certain amount of restyling, such as two-tone paint and cutaway spats, for the Mark VIII's introduction in October 1956. It was also easily distinguished from the Mark VII in that it had a one-piece windscreen rather than one split in the middle. Towards the end of the Mark VIII's relatively short production run, in April 1958, some left-hand-drive versions were fitted with power-assisted steering. This feature, which was popular in America, made the cars much easier to park. It was fitted as standard when the Mark VIII was further developed as the Mark IX in October 1958. The Mark IX was virtually the same as the Mark VIII except that it had the new 3.8-litre XK engine that was to be fitted to the XK150S a year later, and disc brakes all round like the XK150s. The new engine had much more torque than the 3.4-litre unit and greatly improved flexibility, with a good deal of extra performance as well—184 km/h (114.4 mph) maximum speed against 171 km/h (106.5 mph). This was becoming necessary to keep Jaguar's flagship ahead of its American rivals.

The Mark VIII, in 3.4-litre form, continued in production in small numbers alongside the Mark IX until December 1959. However, the Mark IX went on until late in 1961, when it was replaced by the sophisticated new Mark X (described later).

*The Mark IX was the last Jaguar saloon to be built on a separate chassis, carrying its dignified coachwork with great aplomb up to 184 km/h (114 mph)! A proud owner, Graig Hinton, is driving this 1959 model.*

**Jaguar Mark IX (1959)**

**ENGINE**

| | |
|---|---|
| Type | In-line, water-cooled |
| No. of cylinders | 6 |
| Bore/stroke mm | 87 × 106 |
| Displacement cc | 3781 |
| Valve operation | Twin overhead camshafts |
| Sparkplugs per cyl. | 1 |
| Compression ratio | 8:1 (7:1 or 9:1 optional) |
| Carburation | 2 SU 1.75 in carburettors |
| BHP | 210 at 5500 rpm (200 or 220 optional) |

**DRIVE TRAIN**

| | |
|---|---|
| Clutch | Single dry plate |
| Transmission | Automatic |

**CHASSIS**

| | |
|---|---|
| Frame | Box-section girders, cruciform bracing |
| Wheelbase mm | 3048 |
| Track—front mm | 1422 |
| Track—rear mm | 1461 |
| Suspension—front | Independent wishbone and torsion bar |
| Suspension—rear | Live axle, half-elliptic springs |
| Brakes | Girling hydraulic drums |
| Tyre size—front | 6.70 × 16 in |
| Tyre size—rear | 6.70 × 16 in |
| Wheels | 16 in disc |

**PERFORMANCE**

| | |
|---|---|
| Maximum speed | 184 km/h (114 mph) |
| Acceleration | 0–60 mph 11.3 sec, standing quarter mile 18.1 sec |

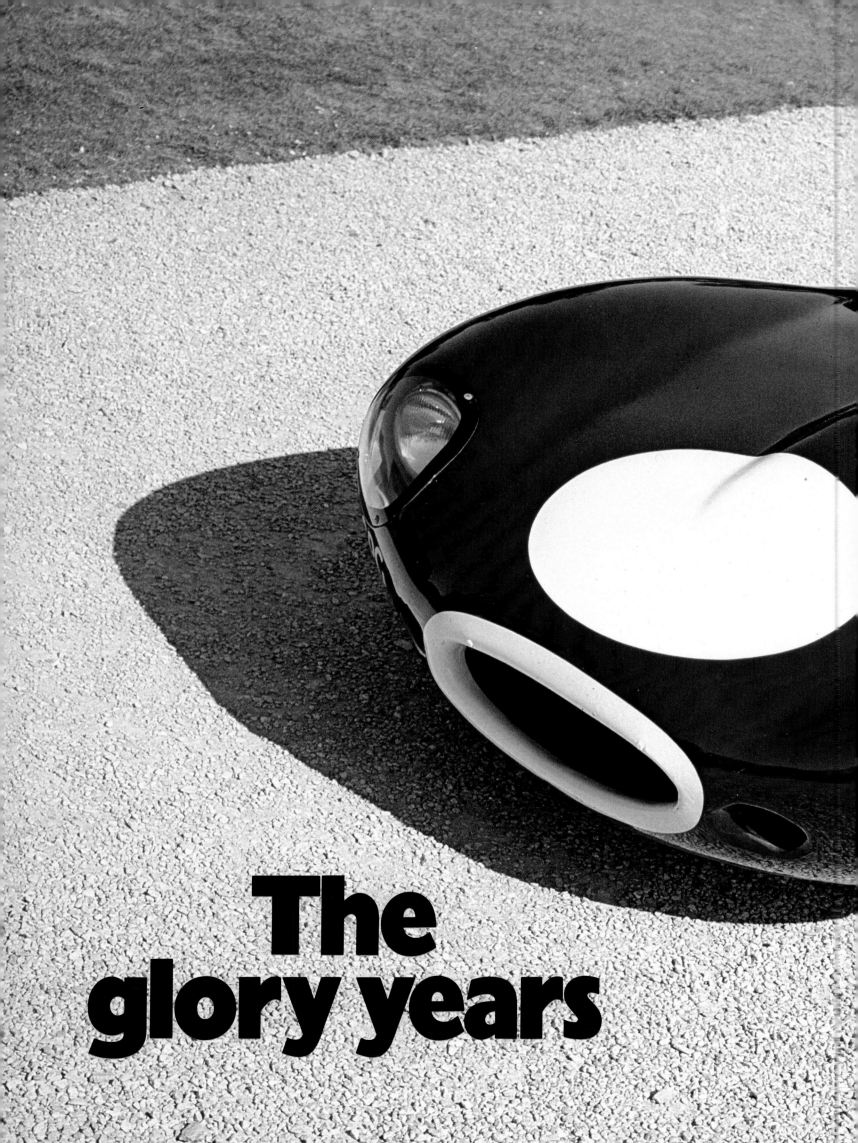

# The glory years

Such was the performance of the XK120 sports car at Le Mans in 1950 that Lyons authorized a special competition version aimed at winning the race in 1951; and because of the pressure of work on developing the Mark VII saloon for production, Heynes and his team found themselves with only six months in which to prepare the competition XK120—the C type—before the great race in June. The extent of their work was incredible in view of the time available. The engine's power was increased by more than 30 per cent to 210 bhp, by means of a new high-compression cylinder head with bigger carburettors and a better exhaust. In addition, a new chassis was designed with torsion-bar rear suspension and the whole car was clothed in a brand-new body! The chassis was very different from the XK120's, being made mainly from tubes to save weight without sacrificing rigidity. The rear suspension was designed with trailing links for better traction than was possible with the standard leaf-spring arrangement. It was lighter and simpler than the popular de Dion racing rear suspension of similar layout and proved inferior only on bumpy roads: but as the C type Jaguar was designed solely to win at Le Mans, this did not matter, for the French circuit had an excellent smooth surface. The beautifully streamlined body reduced drag and featured a front end that lifted up in its entirety for quick and easy maintenance.

Such was the extent of all this development work on the new model that it was touch and go whether it could be made to work properly in time for Le Mans. Therefore Lyons had four XK120s built up with ultra-lightweight bodies as stand-bys in case the new team of C types was not ready. In the event, they were not needed and three of these lightweight XK120s were sold to an American dealer for racing on the West Coast; one was retained by the factory. This was eventually raced by Jaguar publicist Bob Berry, who also campaigned a lightweight Mark VII saloon prepared for, but not used in, the Silverstone Production Car event.

### The C types and HWM-Jaguars on the circuits

Le Mans was a glorious debut for the C type with Moss, Biondetti and Walker occupying the first three places before Biondetti's car came into the pits with the oil-pressure gauge on zero. An oil pipe in the modified sump had fractured in such way that it was obvious the same fate might befall the other two cars, and this is exactly what happened to Moss. But Walker and Peter Whitehead drove on with great smoothness and precision, avoiding a critical vibration period which endangered the engine, to win by some 11 km (7 miles) from the Talbot of Meyrat and Mairesse, with Macklin and Thompson third in an Aston Martin.

Despite the limitations of the C type's rear suspension, Moss won the 1951 Tourist Trophy, with Walker second and Tony Rolt fourth to complete the winning Jaguar team on the bumpy Dundrod circuit. The C types dominated the sports car events they entered as other Jaguar-engined cars began to make their appearance. The most promising was a sports car built by an engineer called John Heath for Phil Scragg. This car used a modified Alta Grand Prix chassis with a highly tuned XK engine and cycle-type wings. It was called the HW-Alta-Jaguar ('HW' after Heath's garage) and became the forerunner of a series of HWM-Jaguars.

In fact, motor trader Oscar Moore had been driving an Alta-engined HWM with some success and then decided to fit a Jaguar engine for the 1952 season. The engine's capacity was increased to 3.8 litres in a similar manner to that eventually adopted by Jaguar (i.e., with liners), rather than by the American method of boring out. In this form, with a body like Scragg's car, Moore's HWM-Jaguar dominated British club racing in 1952.

Jaguar was not content to sit back on its laurels after the Le Mans win and spent a lot of time developing the revolutionary disc braking system. These new brakes overcame the problems associated with the old-fashioned drum brakes and first proved themselves in the Mille Miglia, the classic Italian road race, in 1952. Moss crashed when well placed in the race, but not before he had had time to be impressed by the performance of the new Mercedes 300SLR. In fact, he was so vocal in his appreciation

*RIGHT One of the best-known C types was registered KSF 182, one of seven raced by the Ecurie Ecosse. This car was usually driven by an Army engineer named Jimmy Stewart, who seemed to have an inexhaustible supply of weekend passes because his commanding officer was a racing enthusiast! So was Jimmy's younger brother, Jackie, who went on to become world champion after starting his racing career with an E type. Provided by the Nigel Dawes Collection.*

*PREVIOUS PAGE The glorious long-nosed D type that won the 1955 Le Mans 24-hour race, the first of five built that year for the works and Briggs Cunningham. Displayed in the Midlands Motor Museum.*

**Jaguar C type (1951)**

| | | | |
|---|---|---|---|
| **ENGINE** | | **CHASSIS** | |
| Type | In-line, water-cooled | Frame | Tubular |
| No. of cylinders | 6 | Wheelbase mm | 2438 |
| Bore/stroke mm | 83 × 106 | Track—front mm | 1295 |
| Displacement cc | 3442 | Track—rear mm | 1295 |
| Valve operation | Overhead pushrod | Suspension—front | Independent wishbone |
| Sparkplugs per cyl. | 1 | | and torsion bar |
| Compression ratio | 9 : 1 | Suspension—rear | Live axle, torsion bar |
| Carburation | 2 SU 2 in carburettors | | and trailing arms |
| | or 3 Weber 45DCOE | Brakes | Lockheed hydraulic |
| BHP | 200 at 5800 rpm on | | drum or Dunlop disc |
| | SUs, 230 on Webers | Tyre size—front | 6.00 × 16 in |
| | | Tyre size—rear | 6.50 × 16 in |
| | | Wheels | 16 in wire |
| | | **PERFORMANCE** (road test with SUs) | |
| | | Maximum speed | 230 km/h (143 mph) |
| | | Acceleration | 0–60 mph 8.1 sec, |
| **DRIVE TRAIN** | | | standing quarter mile |
| Clutch | Single dry plate | | 16.2 sec |
| Transmission | Four-speed and reverse | | |

that Jaguar frantically modified the C type's bodywork with a long drooping nose for better air penetration and a higher top speed. Unfortunately, this bodywork caused the engine to overheat and all three cars had to retire ignominiously at Le Mans in 1952. When the standard bodies were refitted, however, the C types promptly won the Rheims 12-hour race. They also competed in the Monaco Grand Prix, which was run for sports cars that year because Formula 1 was in the doldrums. Moss was duelling for the lead with Manzon's Gordini when they crashed at Sainte Dévote corner with several other cars, but Walker's sixth place gave Jaguar its first and last World Championship Grand Prix placing. The C type was also put into limited production that year, and the Scottish Ecurie Ecosse team—which had been running XK120s—was among the first and most successful customers.

Phil Hill and a newcomer called Masten Gregory starred in America as the works cars were prepared for Le Mans, now that teething troubles in the disc brakes had been sorted out. The French race rapidly developed into a duel between Moss and Villoresi in a massive 4.5-litre Ferrari. The Italian car was faster on acceleration, the British car better on braking. Then drama unfolded again as Moss came in with fuel-feed problems. But Rolt and Duncan Hamilton took over to win for Jaguar with Moss and Walker second after their fuel lines had been cleared. It was like a dream come true for the winners, who had been disqualified before the race for an accidental breach of practice regulations, then reinstated when Lyons proved to be at his most persuasive with the race organizers. In between, Rolt and Hamilton had drowned their sorrows and drove the whole 24 hours with monumental hangovers!

Numerous other victories followed all over the world as Heath, and his partner and star driver George Abecassis, continued to do well with all-enveloping bodied HWM-Jaguars. The Ecurie Ecosse carried on with C types, frequently picking up places when the works cars failed or did not enter.

There seemed to be little mechanically that could be improved on the C type for its chief objective, Le Mans, apart from odd points like dry-sump lubrication, which eliminated the oil surge that had ruined the engine's bearings previously. But the body could certainly be improved for a higher top speed.

## The D type

The result of this redesign was one of the most beautiful and charismatic racing sports cars ever made, the D type Jaguar produced for 1954. Its aerodynamic lines, with distinctive tailfin, were largely the work of Malcolm Sayer, who had joined Jaguar from the Bristol Aircraft Company. Although the car retained some kind of tubular chassis, particularly on the first ones built in 1954, the centre section was really a monocoque, like an aircraft fuselage. And in the 1954 Le Mans race it showed itself to be capable of 274 km/h (170 mph)—32 km/h (20 mph) faster than a C type—as it battled for the lead with a team of massive 4.9-litre Ferraris. Once again Moss, partnered by Ken Wharton, was the pacemaker until he was eliminated by various ailments. The Ferraris were suffering, too, and eventually the race developed into a thrilling battle between the Ferrari of Gonzalez and Trintignant, and the D type of Rolt and Hamilton. Towards the end, Gonzalez, the Buenos Aires taxi driver known as the Pampas Bull, had to call on his last reserves of strength to win with the ferocious Ferrari by only a minute from the Jaguar in a glorious second place. After

that, D types won everywhere, especially when they were put into production for 1955. Cooper, the British racing car builders, also made a special with a Jaguar engine for Walker to compete in the same races as the HWM-Jaguars, but it never achieved the same success.

Meanwhile the works cars were further improved with longer-nosed bodywork for better air penetration. In addition some D types appeared without tailfins to save weight and drag on short circuits where the top speed could not be attained, and the straight-line stability imparted by the fin was not needed. Moss was lured away by Mercedes and his place in the works team was taken by rising star Mike Hawthorn. In addition, the well-known sportsman Briggs Cunningham, who had been having tax problems concerning the losses incurred in making his own racing sports cars, formed an American Jaguar team rather like the Ecurie Ecosse. The first results of this partnership were seen when Cunningham's top driver, Phil Walters, won the 1955 Sebring 12-hour race with Hawthorn.

Le Mans was the next big race in 1955 for the works Jaguars, with Hawthorn racing neck and neck with Fangio in a Mercedes. But disaster struck when Levegh's Mercedes collided with Macklin's Austin-Healey in a mix-up involving Hawthorn. The Mercedes disintegrated and pieces fell into the crowd, killing Levegh and 81 other people. Moss took over the leading Mercedes as Ivor Bueb replaced the shocked Hawthorn.

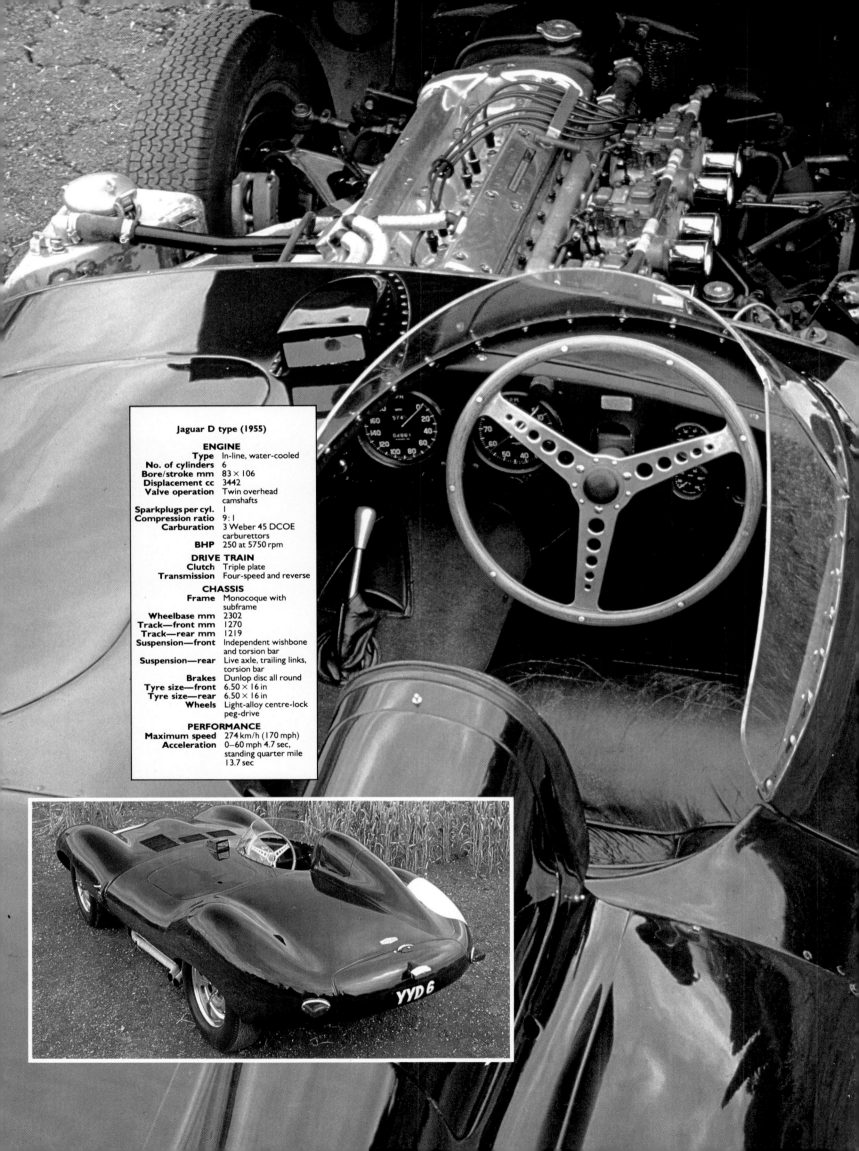

**Jaguar D type (1955)**

**ENGINE**

| | |
|---|---|
| Type | In-line, water-cooled |
| No. of cylinders | 6 |
| Bore/stroke mm | 83 × 106 |
| Displacement cc | 3442 |
| Valve operation | Twin overhead camshafts |
| Sparkplugs per cyl. | 1 |
| Compression ratio | 9 : 1 |
| Carburation | 3 Weber 45 DCOE carburettors |
| BHP | 250 at 5750 rpm |

**DRIVE TRAIN**

| | |
|---|---|
| Clutch | Triple plate |
| Transmission | Four-speed and reverse |

**CHASSIS**

| | |
|---|---|
| Frame | Monocoque with subframe |
| Wheelbase mm | 2302 |
| Track—front mm | 1270 |
| Track—rear mm | 1219 |
| Suspension—front | Independent wishbone and torsion bar |
| Suspension—rear | Live axle, trailing links, torsion bar |
| Brakes | Dunlop disc all round |
| Tyre size—front | 6.50 × 16 in |
| Tyre size—rear | 6.50 × 16 in |
| Wheels | Light-alloy centre-lock peg-drive |

**PERFORMANCE**

| | |
|---|---|
| Maximum speed | 274 km/h (170 mph) |
| Acceleration | 0–60 mph 4.7 sec, standing quarter mile 13.7 sec |

Eventually all close rivals were eliminated before Mercedes withdrew its cars in sympathy for the dead. The D type soldiered on to win an event marred by motor racing's worst accident.

## Jaguar specials
D types continued to race alongside C types in all manner of events as the factory concentrated on developing fuel injection in place of carburation for extra power. Because they had been built for endurance racing, the D and C types were relatively heavy and lightweight specials, such as the HWM-Jaguars, continued to be successful. The Cooper-Jaguars were revised in Mark II form but did not prove to be as competitive as their HWM rivals. Numerous smaller-engined specials were also racing, such as Listers with Bristol and Maserati 2-litre power, and Tojeiros with Bristol units. Of this pair, it was Tojeiro that first entered the bigger classes in 1956 with a Jaguar XK engine.

The Tojeiro car had a very short wheelbase with independent suspension all round and a spaceframe chassis—that is a multi-tube chassis

with more open space than metal to save weight! This ultra-light machine was very fast in a straight line, but difficult to handle in corners. Nevertheless, test pilot Dick Protheroe proved to be highly competitive in this tricky car. Works D types were highly placed in some events, but the Ecurie Ecosse enjoyed more success, particularly when two of the three factory cars crashed at Le Mans and a D type entered by the Scottish team for Ninian Sanderson and Ron Flockhart moved up to win.

The works decided then to retire from racing in 1956 to free Heynes and the development team for work on production cars, and sold its distinctive long-nosed D types to the Ecurie Ecosse. Cunningham also had one, which his ace tuner, Alfred Momo, developed into a 3.8-litre version. Momo's method of increasing the capacity was to be adopted later by the works for production cars. This new 3.8-litre long-nosed D type finished third at Sebring in 1957 in the hands of Hawthorn and Bueb, before going on in fuel-injected form to win at Le Mans for the Ecurie Ecosse with Flockhart and Bueb at the wheel. It was a brilliant year for the D types: another 3.4-litre Ecurie Ecosse car was second, driven by Ninian

| Lister-Jaguar 'knobbly' body (1958) | | CHASSIS | |
|---|---|---|---|
| **ENGINE** | | **Frame** | Twin tube |
| | | **Wheelbase mm** | 2303 |
| **Type** | In-line, water-cooled | **Track—front mm** | 1321 |
| **No. of cylinders** | 6 | **Track—rear mm** | 1359 |
| **Bore/stroke mm** | 87 × 106 | **Suspension—front** | Independent wishbone and coil springs |
| **Displacement cc** | 3781 | **Suspension—rear** | De Dion, trailing arms, coil springs |
| **Valve operation** | Twin overhead camshafts | | |
| | | **Brakes** | Girling discs all round |
| **Sparkplugs per cyl.** | 1 | **Tyre size—front** | 6.00 × 15 in (or 16 in) |
| **Compression ratio** | 9:1 | **Tyre size—rear** | 6.00 × 15 in (or 16 in) |
| **Carburation** | 3 Weber 45 DCOE carburettors | **Wheels** | Light-alloy, centre-lock, peg-drive |
| **BHP** | 295 at 5750 rpm | **PERFORMANCE** | |
| **DRIVE TRAIN** | | **Maximum speed** | Approx. 274 km/h (170 mph) |
| **Clutch** | Triple plate | **Acceleration** | 0–60 mph 4.7 sec, standing quarter mile 13.2 sec |
| **Transmission** | Four-speed and reverse | | |

Sanderson and Johnny Lawrence; a French 3.4-litre D type third for Ralph Lucas and Jean-Marie Brousselot; Paul Frère and Freddy Rousselle fourth in a Belgian 3.4-litre D type; and Duncan Hamilton and Masten Gregory sixth in Hamilton's 3.8-litre D type. 'It was not as though the opposition was weak, except in reliability—and it was our finest hour,' said David Murray, the Edinburgh wine merchant who had sunk everything in his Scottish national racing team.

## The Lister-Jaguars

That year—1957—was also significant in that it marked the début of what was to become by far the most successful Jaguar-engined special, the Lister. The first Lister-Jaguar was a private effort by the London jeweller Norman Hillwood, who fitted a C type engine into a Lister-Bristol chassis. Then Bryan Turle, of BP, persuaded Lister to build a works Jaguar-engined car to combat the Ecurie Ecosse and Aston Martin works teams, both of which were backed by the rival Esso oil company. Jaguar was happy to supply a 3.4-litre dry-sump D type engine in the knowledge that the Lister

works car in the hands of Archie Scott-Brown would present a formidable threat to Aston Martin. In this form, the combination of the ultra-light Lister and Scott-Brown's superb driving ability proved almost unbeatable in British sports car racing that year.

A 3-litre limit was imposed for international sports car racing in 1958 to discourage development of such monsters as the 4.5-litre 450S Maserati after more horrific crashes, particularly in the Mille Miglia. Jaguar reduced the 3.4-litre XK unit to 3 litres, in which form it produced 254 bhp. The new capacity of 2986 cc was achieved by reducing the stroke to 92 mm, but in this form the engine did not prove very reliable. The Ecurie Ecosse's chief tuner, Wilkie Wilkinson, attacked the problem from a different angle, enlarging the 2.4-litre XK engine used in the Mark 1 saloon to 2954 cc by increasing its stroke to 91 mm. With a different crankshaft and connecting

*Lister-Jaguars dominated short-distance circuit races in the late 1950s, and continue to do so in historic events today. This example has the classic 'knobbly' body. Provided by Bobby Bell of Bell and Colvill.*

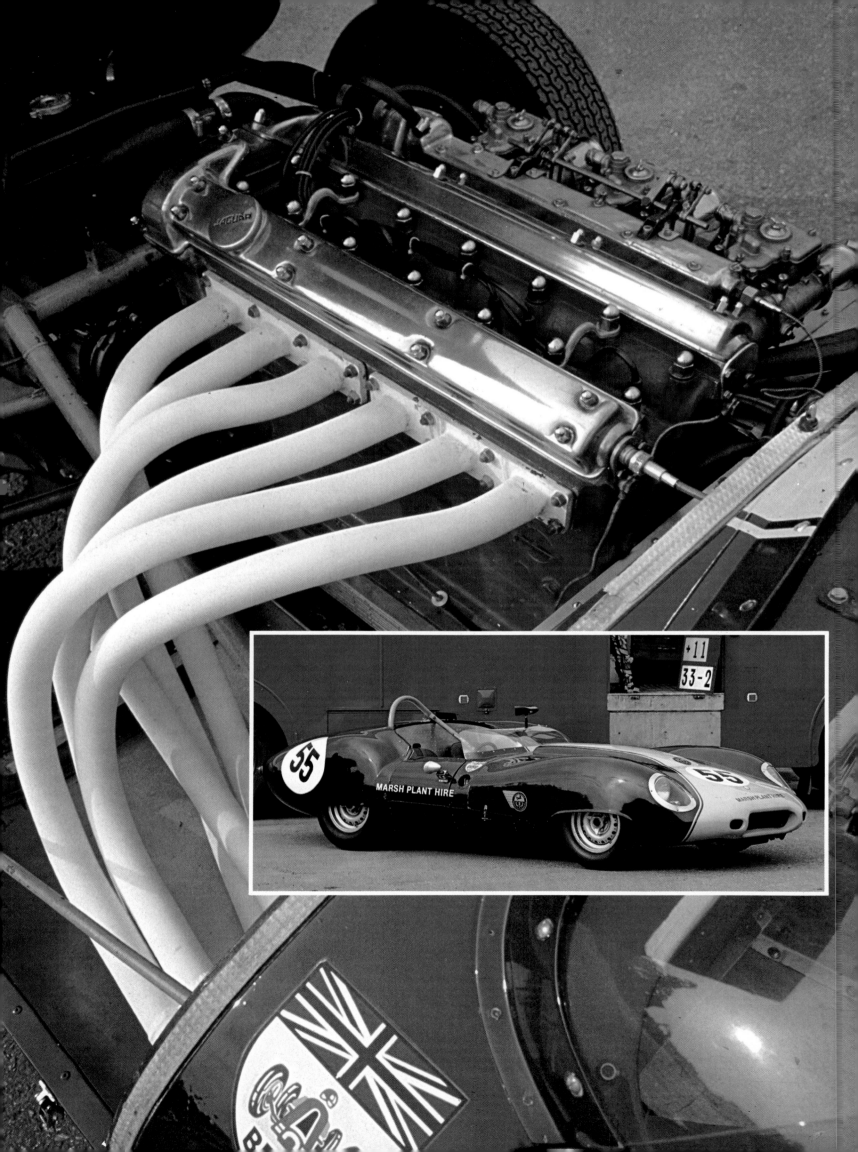

rods, this engine looked as though it would be very reliable, but it produced only 234 bhp, so the Ecurie Ecosse decided to use the works engines in the hope that they would not blow up.

There were no capacity limits in British or American sports car racing, however, so Lister capitalized on this by putting its Jaguar 3.8-litre-engined car into production with a distinctive 'knobbly' body cleverly designed to minimize frontal area by leaving only 'knobs' to cover high points such as the wheels and engine.

The Ecurie Ecosse also decided to experiment with a Lister chassis, but this time in single-seater form for the rich Race of Two Worlds event at Monza, in which the fastest cars from Europe and the United States—regardless of capacity—were invited to compete. Most of the European teams declined because the track was so rough and the potential speeds so high that their cars could not cope. In 1957, the Ecurie Ecosse had survived to take the lion's share of the prizes with its highly placed D types, but felt that there was a chance of winning with a single-seater. So the Scottish team commissioned a Lister-Jaguar, but sadly it proved to be no faster than a D type because of the extra drag imparted by its exposed wheels. The Ecurie also ran a conventional Lister-Jaguar for Gregory with

*ABOVE The E2A prototype pictured at Le Mans in 1960, showing clearly how the E type bonnet was developed.*

*LEFT Listers received bulkier, but more aerodynamic Costin bodies for 1959. This example, driven by Gerry Marshall in historic racing, started life with a Chevrolet engine before receiving an ex-Ecurie Ecosse XK unit. Provided by Geoffrey Marsh of Marsh Plant Hire Ltd.*

*RIGHT Two variants of the lightweight E type are shown in the 1963 Tourist Trophy race at Goodwood. The long-nosed, low-drag version, registered CUT 7, driven by Dick Protheroe, came sixth, and Peter Lumsden's standard-shaped car, registered 49 FXN, finished ninth.*

great success, the American driver proving to be one of the few who could stay with Scott-Brown. In 1958 they were duelling for the lead at Spa when Scott-Brown in the works Lister sadly crashed in flames to his death.

Cunningham re-equipped his team with Lister-Jaguars and Walt Hansgen used them to good effect to win the Sports Car Club of America championships in 1958 and 1959.

Those were the years when the Lister-Jaguars were at their peak, leaving all the other big sports cars trailing. Occasionally they were fitted with the 3-litre XK engine, but usually D types were retained for long-distance events such as Le Mans, where different body regulations applied. The Ecurie Ecosse remained loyal to its D types for Le Mans, but lost both with piston trouble in the first hour in 1958. Bueb and Hamilton lasted

longer, leading during the night, only for Hamilton to crash after 19 hours. Piston trouble struck again in 1959 when the Ecurie Ecosse D type driven by Gregory and Innes Ireland held second or third place behind the leading Aston Martin.

The aerodynamicist Frank Costin was employed to rebody the Lister-Jaguars for 1959, the result being a bulbous creation aimed at reducing drag. However, these new Costin-bodied Listers proved to be no faster overall, partly because their drivers could not judge the corners as accurately as those with 'knobbly' bodied cars.

The Ecurie Ecosse also bought a Tojeiro-Jaguar, racing it alongside the Listers and D type. During 1959 Bueb, who had taken Scott-Brown's place in the Lister team, was killed in a Formula 2 race, and the saddened proprietor, Brian Lister, quit racing. His last design, a spaceframe Lister-Jaguar, was sold with the works cars, which continued to compete successfully in private hands.

### The E2A

Meanwhile, the Jaguar works was experimenting with new prototypes to replace the XK150, eventually building a car that closely resembled a D type, but with independent rear suspension. This suspension was brilliantly simple, like most of Heynes's creations. It used four coil-spring damper units and lower wishbones, with the drive shafts doubling as the top wishbones. Trailing arms located the hub carriers and disc brakes were fitted inboard to reduce unsprung weight for better handling and traction. This new system worked very well and was to form the basis for every Jaguar's rear suspension after that. This particular car, code-named E2A, was lent to Cunningham for the 1960 Le Mans race; it ran well until it was eliminated by piston trouble. Crankshaft problems, for a change, sidelined the Ecurie Ecosse's grand old D type, driven by Flockhart and Bruce Halford. The Jaguar E2A was especially significant, however, in that it was a direct forerunner of the E type sports car, described later, and was similar in construction to the lightweight competition E types of the 1960s.

### Competition E types and specials

As Lister-Jaguars continued to be competitive in club events and some internationals, Jaguar was developing its steel-bodied E type production car. It was only natural that, when these started leaving the factory in quantity in 1961, they would be used in production sports car racing. These cars, with 3.8-litre engines, were quite successful, but by 1962 they were being consistently outpaced by exotic Ferraris costing four times as

much. So the teams running E types, particularly that of Surrey dealer John Coombs, started lightening their cars as much as possible. The Coombs E type, registered 4 WPD, was in effect a factory experimental car and formed the basis for the first of the lightweight competition E types with alloy monocoques, like the E2A and the D types, rather than steel shells like production E types. For Protheroe, one of these lightweight E types was fitted with a special low-drag fixed-head body, which amounted to the final development of Sayer's D and E type shape. These cars were raced with some success, particularly a team operated by Cunningham at Le Mans in 1963. But the most successful was that of the German distributor Peter Lindner, whose alloy-blocked 3.8-litre XK unit developed up to 344 bhp. The spaceframe Lister-Jaguar was also raced by Peter Sargent at Le Mans with a Costin fixed-head body.

The ex-Briggs Cunningham lightweight E type which finished ninth at Le Mans in 1963 is shown with its competition modifications, including Le Mans wheel arch extensions, fuel injection engine, rear-end vents for letting hot air out of the cockpit, and modified inboard brakes and differential. Provided by the Nigel Dawes Collection.

## The experimental XJ13

Far more specialized mid-engined cars with wider wheels which could not be used on the road were taking over sports car racing by 1964, and the basically production E types were being rendered uncompetitive. The Jaguar factory, however, had been experimenting with a V12-cylinder engine since 1955, and began thinking again in 1964 about Le Mans. The engine they had in mind was a four overhead camshaft unit with two banks of cylinders at an angle of 60 degrees to each other. The bore and stroke of 70 mm by 87 mm gave a capacity of 4994 cc, producing more than 500 bhp at 7600 rpm. This alloy unit was fitted into an advanced mid-engined monocoque body that strongly resembled a D type's in construction and detail appearance. The suspension was similar in many ways to that of an E type and a ZF five-speed gearbox, which had been used in some of the lightweight E types, was employed. This car, called the XJ13, was completed in 1966 and could have been used at Le Mans that year. But by then, Jaguar was deeply involved in amalgamation with the British Motor Corporation, and any plans for Le Mans were disrupted. Testing showed that the XJ13 could have remained competitive until the late 1960s, but development was curtailed when it became apparent that many changes would have had to be made to accommodate new tyre technology. There was also the feeling that the sight and sound of a Jaguar V12 engine might have had a bad effect on the sales of the existing six-cylinder cars as potential customers saved their money for a new car that was still many years away from production reality.

The glorious old C and D types, and Jaguar specials, continued to circulate in club events until they took on a new lease of life in historic racing during the 1970s. Today the Lister-Jaguars are as dominant as ever in these events, most of which are run over the relatively short distances they excelled at in their heyday.

*Jaguar's mid-engined prototype sports racing car, the XJ13, shown here at Silverstone's Copse Corner, could have raced against the might of Ford and Ferrari at Le Mans in 1966 had more time been available for development. As it stands it is a reminder of what glory might have been achieved. Provided by Jaguar Cars Ltd.*

# E type
# extravaganza

The E type Jaguar that replaced the XK150 in 1961 caused a similar sensation to the original XK120 in 1948. It was quite simply the fastest and most spectacular sports car available to the general public. It was also far ahead of its competitors in that it was based on well-tried components that gave it a rugged reliability. The steel monocoque, which closely resembled that of the alloy D type in its roadster form, was also made with a sleek fixed head; the bonnet was similar to the one on the long-nosed D type with small bumpers reminiscent of those on the XK120, and later ones fitted to a few road-going versions of the D type called the XKSS. The XKSS was exactly the same as the production D type except that it was equipped with tiny slim-line bumpers, a full-width windscreen, silencers and lighting suitable for road use. Some of the very few XKSSs were even fitted with a luggage rack for touring! The object of producing this very fast model in 1957 was to use a surplus of D type parts rather than to launch a car to be produced in quantity.

The E type was the production reality. Its interior was lighter and simpler than the XK150's but the engine and gearbox were the same as in the 3.8-litre XK150S, except that there was insufficient room for the optional overdrive or an automatic transmission. Roadster versions of the E type were available with an optional hard top that followed established Jaguar lines. The front suspension was mounted on a subframe bolted to the scuttle in the same way as the later D types, and was traditional Jaguar in its torsion-bar layout. But the rear suspension was now independent, and based on the layout used on the E2A prototype. Wire wheels and disc brakes all round were fitted as standard on this rakish and astonishing machine. Apart from its extraordinarily low basic price of £1600, what stuck in most people's minds was the fantastic performance—240 km/h (150 mph) on road test with a 0–60 mph acceleration time of only 6.8 seconds, and a fuel consumption of 16.6 litres/100 km (17 mpg). Not only did the E type perform well and sell at an amazingly modest price, but it also looked far more attractive than any of its rivals: a true Jaguar.

### Early sales and competition successes
As could only be expected, the E type, in both fixed-head and open forms, was an immediate sales success, particularly in Jaguar's main export market, the United States. And like the XK120, it won its first race—at Oulton Park in April 1961! Graham Hill's Equipe Endeavour E type led

48

*ABOVE The missing link between the D and E type—Bryan Corser's lovely XKSS, which started life as a production D type in 1955, chassis number XKD540. It was converted to an XKSS at Browns Lane in 1957 at the request of its first owner, Phil Scragg.*

*PREVIOUS PAGES AND RIGHT First registered in 1962, this is one of the early 3.8-litre fixed-head E types. It is standard except for D type camshafts, competition clutch and a lightened flywheel for racing. Provided by Graham Bovet-White and here driven by his father, Derek.*

home Innes Ireland in an Aston Martin DB4GT, with Roy Salvadori third in another E type entered by John Coombs. This car was registered BUY 1, although later in the year that distinctive number was transferred to another Coombs machine. The E type was then re-registered 4 WPD to become the first of the lightweights. Scores of early successes followed for the E types, culminating in Salvadori's fourth place at Le Mans in 1962 in a car shared with Cunningham. Sargent and Peter Lumsden were fifth in their E type, which was eventually to be developed into a Sayer-style low-drag coupé before they switched to the spaceframe Lister-Jaguar.

Protheroe was one of the first and most successful E type racers. He had a coupé registered CUT 7 before he sold it to Roger Mac and continued with the original Sayer low-drag coupé. As the lightweight E types entered the forefront of international competition, the more standard cars continued to enjoy success in all manner of events. Merle Brennan, in the United States, proved almost unbeatable in Sports Car Club of America (SCCA) races between 1962 and 1964. Later E types starred in the modified sports car racing of the late 1960s and early 1970s before finding their way into today's historic car events. The E type was to become one of Jaguar's most popular, and certainly most distinctive, cars.

### Development of the E type power unit
When the big saloons described in the next chapter needed more torque, the 3.8-litre engine's capacity was increased to 4.2 litres by using a bigger bore of 92.07 mm, with the existing 106 mm stroke. In this form the 4235 cc engine gave the same 265 bhp but had seven per cent more torque. Performance was slightly down because the XK engine in its 4.2-litre form could not rev quite as fast with reliability as the earlier 3.8-litre.

**Jaguar E type roadster (1965)**

### ENGINE

| | |
|---|---|
| Type | In-line, water-cooled |
| No. of cylinders | 6 |
| Bore/stroke mm | 92 × 106 |
| Displacement cc | 4235 |
| Valve operation | Twin overhead camshafts |
| Sparkplugs per cyl. | I |
| Compression ratio | 9 : I |
| Carburation | 3 SU 2 in carburettors |
| BHP | 265 at 5500 rpm |

### DRIVE TRAIN

| | |
|---|---|
| Clutch | Single dry plate |
| Transmission | Four-speed and reverse |

### CHASSIS

| | |
|---|---|
| Frame | Monocoque with subframes |
| Wheelbase mm | 2438 |
| Track—front mm | 1270 |
| Track—rear mm | 1270 |
| Suspension—front | Independent wishbone and torsion bar |
| Suspension—rear | Independent wishbone and coil, radius arms |
| Brakes | Dunlop disc all round |
| Tyre size—front | 6.40 × 15 in |
| Tyre size—rear | 6.40 × 15 in |
| Wheels | 15 in knock-off wire |

### PERFORMANCE

| | |
|---|---|
| Maximum speed | 241 km/h (150 mph) |
| Acceleration | 0–60 mph 6.8 sec, standing quarter mile 15 sec |

*Two of the most beautiful E types in Britain are owned by Will Athawes. His 1965 roadster and fixed-head coupé show the similarity in their lines. The roadster (featured in the main photograph) has won many concours awards.*

But that change cost only about 8 km/h (5 mph) on top speed. This development of the E type engine, which went into production on all models from October 1964, was allied to a much-improved new all-synchromesh gearbox, in common with Jaguar's contemporary saloons.

In March 1966, the wheelbase of the fixed-head car was stretched from 2438 mm (8 ft) to 2667 mm (8 ft 9 in) and the roof raised to make way for XK150-style rear seats. The original fixed-head bodyshape continued in production with two seats only as did the roadster, the new model being known as the 2 plus 2. The increase in wheelbase also allowed sufficient room for automatic transmission to be offered as an option. The extra weight and bulk of this variant of the E type brought its top speed down towards the 210 km/h (130 mph) mark, but it soon became popular with customers requiring more room, particularly in the United States.

## North American restrictions and the series two cars
Safety and emission regulations began to dictate the shape of cars bought by Americans during the mid-1960s—and not always for the better. Jaguar had to cater for these changes, some of which were so extensive that they would not have been economical had they been introduced purely on North American export models. As a result, the E type's enclosed headlights had to be elevated slightly and exposed in 1967. This, together with other less obvious alterations, and the addition of power-sapping anti-emission devices on North American-specification cars, changed the model's appearance. These were the cars with the original E type slim radiator air intake and exposed headlights that were to become known by enthusiasts everywhere as the 'series 1½'; the original pre-1967 cars became the 'series one'; and later models with a much larger air intake and similar exposed headlights were called, officially this time, the series two.

*ABOVE LEFT The E type fixed-head coupé was 'stretched' in 1966 to make the 2 plus 2. The distinctive high roofline can be seen clearly here. Provided by Tony and Pat Dudmesh.*

*LEFT The original E type, later called the series one to distinguish it from updated models, was revised constantly during 1967 to meet ever-changing US regulations. This is a 'series 1½' model with series one features such as triple windscreen wipers, but with open headlamps like the later cars. It has covered only 400 km (250 miles) from new, having spent its early years on display in the* Queen Elizabeth *ocean liner. Provided by Jaguar Cars Ltd.*

*BELOW The series two E type introduced in 1968 combined the series 1½ features with many new ones. Provided by Hills Sports Car Centre.*

These series two cars, introduced in October 1968, besides the larger radiator air intake, had twin electric fans because of the anti-pollution equipment, which had to be fitted in even more strangulating form to North American-specification cars. These devices had the dual effect of making the engine run hotter, and therefore better under-bonnet air circulation was needed. They also reduced the amount of power that could be used and as a result the performance of the E types dropped to between 210 km/h (130 mph) and 217 km/h (135 mph), depending on specification. But they remained one of the fastest ranges of sports cars on the road because everyone else's products had suffered too. Some of the Jaguar's rivals, such as Austin-Healey with its 3-litre sports car, had to stop making them altogether because of the severity of the new regulations in such an important market as the United States.

The constant sapping of the power of the XK engine also meant that the introduction of the new V12 became more imperative, especially as the saloon cars that shared units similar to the E type would also benefit from the extra potential power to keep them ahead of the opposition.

As development work progressed on the engine—one of the main problems was getting it to run sufficiently cool in the restricted confines of a Jaguar's bonnet—the series two E types continued to be modified principally to meet American regulations, which were becoming more and more severe. Automatic transmission and pressed-steel wheels also became optional as the anti-smog controls reduced power from the 246 bhp of the series 1½ to 177 bhp for the last of the series two models. Consequently the E type assumed a 'softer' image. By 1971 the V12 engine, which was also to be introduced in the new range of XJ saloons, was ready for production and, as with the XK engine of 1948, it was tried in the lower-volume sports model first.

## The V12 power unit
The new V12 engine used an alloy cylinder block like its prototype in the XJ13 sports-racing car. This kept down the weight to not much more than the XK unit and meant that the suspension and bodyshell of the existing cars did not have to be modified very much, and the engine could be sited reasonably well forward without upsetting the car's balance. The alloy block also dispersed heat more efficiently, but in its original form, with four overhead camshafts, it was far too wide to allow the front wheels to turn sufficiently to give an acceptable parking lock. With this in mind, and in the interests of economy of production, a single overhead camshaft was substituted on each cylinder block. This reduced the power available in a reliable state of road tune to around 300 bhp, which was not much more than had been available with the XK unit before emission controls. Consequently the capacity of the V12 was increased to 5343 cc by using a bore of 90 mm and a stroke of 70 mm, which gave a power output of

**Jaguar E type V12 roadster (1972)**

**ENGINE**

| | |
|---|---|
| Type | Vee, water-cooled |
| No. of cylinders | 12 |
| Bore/stroke mm | 90 × 70 |
| Displacement cc | 5343 |
| Valve operation | Single overhead camshaft |
| Sparkplugs per cyl. | 1 |
| Compression ratio | 9:1 |
| Carburation | 4 Zenith 175 CDSE carburettors |
| BHP | 272 at 5850 rpm |

**DRIVE TRAIN**

| | |
|---|---|
| Clutch | Single dry plate |
| Transmission | Four-speed and reverse (automatic optional) |

**CHASSIS**

| | |
|---|---|
| Frame | Monocoque with subframes |
| Wheelbase mm | 2667 |
| Track—front mm | 1384 |
| Track—rear mm | 1346 |
| Suspension—front | Independent wishbone and torsion bar |
| Suspension—rear | Independent wishbone and coil, radius arms |
| Brakes | Girling discs all round |
| Tyre size—front | E70VR-15 |
| Tyre size—rear | E70VR-15 |
| Wheels | 15 in × 6K wire or solid |

**PERFORMANCE**

| | |
|---|---|
| Maximum speed | 235 km/h (146 mph) |
| Acceleration | 0–60 mph 6.4 sec, standing quarter mile 14.2 sec |

325 bhp on the old standards and 272 bhp on new requirements that were being adopted generally at about the time the new engine was introduced. Careful attention was paid to manifolding and induction, with the use of four Zenith carburettors and Lucas electronic ignition. In this form the V12 engine met the most stringent American exhaust emission regulations and transformed the E type to give a performance more like that of the original 1961 3.8-litre cars.

This was achieved despite extensive changes to the bodyshell, which increased the car's weight and drag. The longer wheelbase was adopted for all E types, whether they were open or closed. This meant that the fixed-head model assumed the shape of the old 2 plus 2 and the new roadster was much longer than originally, with a new optional hardtop as well. The new roadster retained its original, but enlarged, two-seater cockpit, with a big parcel shelf behind the front seats where the new fixed-head's rear seats were located. The E type's bonnet was further modified with an even larger radiator air intake to reduce the extra heat generated by the 5.3-litre engine. Much-improved brakes were adopted with wider wheels, which necessitated flared wheel arches to cope with the improved performance. Although the new V12 engine was not much heavier than the old XK unit, it was enough to make manual steering impossible and a power-assisted system like the one used on the new XJ saloon car range was fitted as standard. With improved torque and a remarkably smooth engine, plus the extra room in the cockpit and the new steering, the new E types—called the series three—felt far more like sporting saloons than the original, which was so closely aligned to the D type. But the series three E type could perform really well and achieved great sales success, because its price was kept down to established Jaguar standards.

*PREVIOUS PAGES The series three E type was the first Jaguar to use the new V12 engine (inset). It also used the long wheelbase bodyshell as standard. This roadster, fitted with a detachable hard top, has been a frequent concours winner. Provided by Alan Hames.*

## E types in modsports and prodsports

By 1972, modified sports car races (modsports), which had been dominated by E types, were becoming too expensive for the amateurs they were intended to attract, and the cars too far removed from anything that could be driven on the road. Consequently there was a revival in Britain of prodsports (production sports car racing), from which modsports had been derived. Eligible cars were divided into price categories and the series three E type was ideal for the class up to £3000. In fact, it was also so fast that it was a potential overall winner, despite the presence of cars costing more than twice as much. Jaguar development engineer Peter Taylor ably demonstrated this by winning the first of the new prodsports championships in 1973. In modsports racing, Guy Beddington continued to thrill the crowds with a fuel-injection series three E type that was astonishingly fast but lacked good brakes! Then, in America, a driver called Bob Tullius managed to persuade British Leyland—which had been formed following the Jaguar-British Motor Corporation amalgamation—that racing a V12 E type would give a fillip to sales in the same way as Brennan's success had done in the mid-1960s. The suggestion appealed to British Leyland because of the excellent track record of Tullius's East Coast-based Group 44 team, which had specialized in British cars for years; and also because their programme could be linked to that of Huffaker Engineering on the West Coast, who had run Brennan's car among other Jaguars. Development engineers such as Taylor helped with test data and within six months the SCCA series three E types were ready to compete in 1974 events. They dominated B production events with Tullius in the Group 44 car and Lee Mueller in the Huffaker machine.

Back in Britain the E types continued in production until the end of 1974, when looming American crash regulations meant that they had to be abandoned. Sales continued well into 1975 as the motoring world went through a slump generated by the 1974 oil crisis. It was a great pity that it faded away because Jaguar was never able to replace the glorious E type, although the production lines were to be occupied by a new Grand Touring car using the same engine and transmission, the XJ-S (see p. 75).

ABOVE *The Jaguar Drivers' Club—with president Mike Cooper's car in the foreground at Dover—organized a trip to Switzerland in 1981 to commemorate the E type's introduction at the 1961 Geneva Show.*

BELOW *Few of the longer, heavier series three E types have been raced, but one, the Group 44 car of Bob Tullius, was highly successful in Sports Car Club of America Group B events. Provided by Jaguar Cars Ltd.*

# The businessman's express

The success of the sports cars and the extraordinary performance of the Mark VII saloon established Jaguar's world-wide reputation for highly desirable cars that offered exceptional value for money. Of course, not everyone wanted a two-seater, nor indeed a six-seater. Most customers wanted something in between: a compact saloon with four or five seats and the same Jaguar performance, opulence and value for money. Happily, Jaguar was able to give them just what they wanted in 1955: the Mark 1 saloon. This delightful 2.4-litre car was designed from the start with an eye to economy, but such was its potential that it was soon given the larger 3.4-litre engine to make it one of the fastest saloon cars in the world. It was then developed into what many people consider the greatest Jaguar of them all: the Mark 2 saloon of 1959. To discerning enthusiasts this certainly became the definitive Jaguar and it formed the basis for the more sophisticated saloons to follow: the large Mark X, and the smaller S types, and the Daimler variants when that long-established Coventry car maker was taken over by Jaguar. In the 1950s the concept of these Jaguars and Daimlers was so successful that they not only dominated their class for general sales, but swept all before them in production saloon car racing and provided the heart and soul of the Daimler Limousine—a car that is still in production as a favourite means of transport for dignitaries and diplomats.

## The Mark 1 and the unitary bodyshell

In the 1950s the Mark 1 saloon's unitary method of construction was a new venture for Jaguar. This type of body—in which the basic shell doubled as the chassis—had an advantage in that it saved weight and was inherently more rigid. This was because the old-fashioned chassis, such as that used in the Mark VII saloon, was always a compromise because its weight had to be kept within reasonable bounds. This meant that it could not have sufficient bracing to make it really rigid. And because it tended to be whippy, the suspension did not work as well as it should have done. The body, which was bolted on to the chassis, helped to stiffen it, but not so much as a properly designed unit combining the functions of the chassis with the extra stiffening produced by the bodyshell. Stress engineering for cars was in its infancy in the 1950s, so the Jaguar Mark 1's bodyshell tended to be, if anything, too strong and heavy, but it was still much more efficient than the older system. The problem of the whippy chassis had been attacked from a different direction on the C type sports car by using

*ABOVE The 2.4-litre Mark 1 Jaguar saloon enjoyed a new lease of life when classic saloon car racing started in 1976. This ex-works car won Group B in this series in 1976 and 1977.*

*RIGHT The 2.4-litre saloon was Jaguar's first unitary-construction compact car, setting new standards of performance and economy without sacrificing comfort. This 1955 Mark 1 model has been fitted with the popular late-style rear wheel spats.*

*PREVIOUS PAGES Jaguars have always been famous for the magnificence of their interiors, particularly the instrument panel. This is from the largest of them all, the 420G. All three cars provided by Graig Hinton.*

| Jaguar Mark 1 2.4-litre (1955) | |
|---|---|
| **ENGINE** | |
| Type | In-line, water-cooled |
| No. of cylinders | 6 |
| Bore/stroke mm | 83 × 76.5 |
| Displacement cc | 2483 |
| Valve operation | Twin overhead camshafts |
| Sparkplugs per cyl. | 1 |
| Compression ratio | 8:1 (7:1 optional) |
| Carburation | 2 Solex carburettors |
| BHP | 112 at 5750 rpm |
| **DRIVE TRAIN** | |
| Clutch | Single dry plate |
| Transmission | Four-speed and reverse (automatic optional) |
| **CHASSIS** | |
| Frame | Integral |
| Wheelbase mm | 2677 |
| Track—front mm | 1387 |
| Track—rear mm | 1273 |
| Suspension—front | Independent wishbone and coil |
| Suspension—rear | Live axle, cantilever, Panhard rod, half-elliptic leaf springs |
| Brakes | Dunlop disc all round |
| Tyre size—front | 6.40 × 15 in |
| Tyre size—rear | 6.40 × 15 in |
| Wheels | 15 in disc |
| **PERFORMANCE** | |
| Maximum speed | 163 km/h (101 mph) |
| Acceleration | 0–60 mph 14.4 sec, standing quarter mile 19.6 sec |

a frame made up of tubes and bulkheads. This, too, was very rigid, but would have been impractical for use on a mass-production saloon car. Elements of the D type's aircraft-style monocoque were contained in the Mark 1's bodyshell. They both used a subframe—although of vastly different design—to mount the front suspension, and utilized massive tubular sills for body rigidity. Jaguar was worred about rigidity when designing the Mark 1 bodyshell. Very thick pillars were used to support the roof, which was an essential stressed component, and a sunroof was never fitted, although the bigger saloons had them as standard. As it happened, the Mark 1's bodyshell was so stiff that it was not seriously weakened by cutting a hole in the top for a sunroof, and this feature became a popular non-standard fitting. Jaguar was also concerned that the Mark 1 might be too noisy, because unitary bodyshells often acted like steel drums when noise and vibration were fed into them. For this reason, everything that might transmit these unwelcome factors was attached to the bodyshell by rubber blocks.

Naturally, this new bodyshell did not abandon all resemblance to the older separate-chassis system. It still had two channel sections running from the front to the rear wheel arches. The steel floor and transverse members were welded to this to form a rigid platform. The scuttle and rear seat pan were welded to this structure with well-reinforced roof supports, and the roof itself formed the top of the box. The outer body was then welded on to the structure for even greater rigidity.

With such a stiff basis to the car, relatively soft suspension could be used, which paid dividends in ride and roadholding. The front suspension was similar to that of the Mark VII saloon, except that it used coil springs rather than torsion bars. This was because Jaguar was not confident that the bodyshell would be strong enough to take the stress of the rear anchorage of the torsion bars. The tops of the coil springs were mounted in turrets on the engine bay sides, with the rest of the suspension on a subframe, which also carried the steering gear. The rear suspension used normal half-elliptic springs turned upside down with one end attached to the live rear axle and the front half clamped to the bodyshell so that they acted, in effect, as quarter-elliptic springs. These were used because Jaguar was not sure that the rear end of the body—behind the front of the wheel arches—was sufficiently strong to take the suspension loads. Had the perimeter channel sections been extended back that far, they might as well have used a separate chassis. An adjustable Panhard rod stopped the axle moving sideways and trailing arms prevented it from twisting under power.

### The Mark 1 and the Mark VII compared
All the basic dimensions on the Mark 1 were smaller than those of the Mark VII, especially the engine, which was a 2.4-litre version of the XK unit. This reduction in capacity, aimed at economy, was achieved by reducing the stroke to 76.5 mm, which enabled the engine to rev faster and helped to make up for some of the power lost by the capacity reduction. The original XK cylinder head—retrospectively called the A type—was used with twin Solex carburettors, rather than SU, to save petrol at the expense of all-out performance. Nevertheless, the 2.4-litre Mark 1 was still capable of 154 km/h (96 mph). A notable feature of its outward appearance was that the dictates of aerodynamics and styling meant that it had to have a teardrop shape—as viewed from above—and rear wheel spats. Thus the rear axle had to be 114 mm (4.5 in) narrower than the front so that the rear wheels could be contained within the

*LEFT Jaguar dominated saloon car racing in the 1950s and early 1960s with first the Mark VII and then the Mark I in 3.4-litre form. But the greatest of them all was the 3.8-litre Mark 2, two examples of which are seen here cornering in their inimitable manner. They often used wire wheels to help cool their hard-pressed brakes.*

*BELOW The standard steel wheels were quite adequate for road use, and much easier to keep clean, particularly when fitted with these aluminium trims. The 3.8-litre Mark 2 saloon shown here also has a full-length Webasto sunroof. Provided by Graig Hinton.*

teardrop shape and spats. This feature was frequently blamed for alleged instability at high speed, although the weight distribution of 55 per cent front and 45 per cent rear had more to do with that. It must be stressed that this instability was only alleged: there was no mention of it in any contemporary road tests and no sign of it when the cars were seen in competition.

The trim of the new Mark I saloon was finished to the same high standards as the contemporary Mark VIIM, but fanatical attention to detail ensured that there was no wastage of material; and, with Lyons's confidence that the basic design would be in production for many years, its price was kept down to only 80 per cent of the larger Jaguar. The accent was on economy, and an optional overdrive was offered to make high-speed cruising more relaxed and economical. This option proved to be popular and, of the two models listed, the slightly more expensive Special Equipment version with rev counter, foglights, heater and so on, immediately outsold the more austere Standard model. In fact, very few

### Jaguar Mark 2 3.8-litre (1962)

#### ENGINE

| | |
|---|---|
| Type | In-line, water-cooled |
| No. of cylinders | 6 |
| Bore/stroke mm | 87 × 106 |
| Displacement cc | 3781 |
| Valve operation | Twin overhead camshafts |
| Sparkplugs per cyl. | 1 |
| Compression ratio | 9 : 1 |
| Carburation | 2 SU 1.75 in carburettors |
| BHP | 220 at 5500 rpm |

#### DRIVE TRAIN

| | |
|---|---|
| Clutch | Single dry plate |
| Transmission | Four-speed and reverse (automatic optional) |

#### CHASSIS

| | |
|---|---|
| Frame | Integral |
| Wheelbase mm | 2677 |
| Track—front mm | 1397 |
| Track—rear mm | 1356 |
| Suspension—front | Independent wishbone and coil |
| Suspension—rear | Live axle, cantilever, Panhard rod, half-elliptic leaf springs |
| Brakes | Dunlop disc all round |
| Tyre size—front | 6.40 × 15 in |
| Tyre size—rear | 6.40 × 15 in |
| Wheels | 15 in knock off wire or disc |

#### PERFORMANCE

| | |
|---|---|
| Maximum speed | 201 km/h (125 mph) |
| Acceleration | 0–60 mph 8.5 sec, standing quarter mile 16.3 sec |

Standard models were made, which tended to show that perhaps Lyons had underestimated the amount of money that people were willing to spend on a compact Jaguar saloon.

Because it was relatively heavy at 1372 kg (3024 lb), and the power output of the 2.4-litre engine was modest, the early Mark I saloon tended to be overshadowed by the Mark VII in competition, although Frank Grounds gave it an early success by finishing fourth in the RAC Rally in 1956, and soon after Frère won the Spa Production Car Race in a Mark I. Even Hamilton in his Mark I could not keep up with the Mark VIIs or Wharton's much-modified Austin A90 in the Silverstone Production Car Race that year. But there was nothing that could touch the Mark I in saloon car racing after it had received the 3.4-litre engine in March 1957. The larger unit was not really installed to make the Mark I a racing machine but rather to appease the American customers who could not understand why Jaguar did not use its most powerful engine in this car. Economy was of little importance to them in those days of very cheap fuel. Jaguar had tried offering various stages of tuning equipment to boost the power of the 2.4-litre unit, but these optional extras put up the price almost to that of the new Mark VIII. As a result, the vast majority of American customers chose the six-seater saloon, particularly because it was offered with the option of automatic transmission.

## The 3.4-litre Mark I
The fitting of the 3.4-litre engine with automatic transmission available involved a considerable number of changes to the Mark I, which is why Lyons had been reluctant to offer it in this form from the outset. The power unit was exactly the same as the one fitted to the Mark VIII saloon, complete with B type cylinder head, SU carburettors and twin exhausts, linked to the same manual or automatic gearbox. The rear axle was strengthened by incorporating Mark VIII components and a larger radiator was fitted to cope with the extra heat generated by the bigger engine. This meant that the front of the car had to be restyled to accommodate a wider radiator grille, similar to the one fitted to the XK150 sports car. The new frontal appearance was standardized on the 2.4-litre Mark I six months later, in conjunction with cutaway rear spats, which were fitted to the 3.4-litre Mark I to help brake cooling. Very early 3.4-litre Mark I saloons had the same drum brakes as the 2.4-litre, but these proved to be inadequate when the maximum performance was achieved: up to a 193 km/h (120 mph) top speed with a 0–60 mph time of 9.1 seconds. As a result, disc brakes like those on the XK150 sports car were offered as an option almost immediately. These were such an improvement that few 3.4-litre Mark I saloons left the factory with drum brakes. As a result of its unitary construction the new saloon weighed little more than the 2.4-litre, and only 51 kg (112 lb) more than the XK150. Because of this, its performance was on a par with the sports car, a fact that was ably demonstrated by Hawthorn, Bueb and Hamilton, who finished first, second and third in the 1957 Silverstone Production Car Race in 3.4-litre Mark I works cars with disc brakes. Scott-Brown challenged for the lead with a private 3.4-litre Mark I until its drum brakes faded too badly for him to continue.

## Mark I racing and rallying successes
This was the start of seven years of Jaguar dominance in saloon car racing and fast rallies such as the Tour de France. Various optional extras were introduced, such as a limited-slip differential, to improve the Mark I's performance in competition, although the cars remained almost standard—a great tribute to their design and construction. The only weak point that became readily apparent was in the Panhard rod mounting; this was strengthened to cope with the stresses of high-speed cornering, which increased as tyres were improved.

The Tour de France was particularly important for Jaguar fortunes in that it represented an ultimate test of fast road and circuit work. Several private entrants received works backing now that the factory had withdrawn from competition with the D types. Initially, the Tour de France had been weighted in favour of sports cars, but the categories were revised in 1957 to make the event, in effect, a competition for two classes of car: Grand Touring, in which Ferraris were dominant, and touring. It was in the touring class that Jaguar was to excel with the 3.4-litre Mark I. Bad luck eliminated early leaders such as Hernano da Silva Ramos, Sir Gawaine Baillie and Bernard Consten in 1957; troubles that were to be repeated in 1958 although Baillie took third place. But da Silva Ramos won in 1959 to give Jaguar the first of a string of successes.

Tommy Sopwith, Baillie's team leader and manager of the Equipe Endeavour, won numerous circuit races with his 3.4-litre Mark I in 1957

and 1958. Baillie was frequently second, with the toughest opposition coming from a similar car entered by Coombs which was usually driven by Hamilton or Flockhart. However, because of the extensive works support it received Hansgen, Cunningham's star driver, used it for a guest appearance at Silverstone in 1958. The American driver won when Sopwith lost a wheel, which highlighted some of the problems facing racing saloon car drivers in this period. At the time purpose-built competition wheels were not allowed in these events, so cars often lost their highly stressed standard wheels. Jaguar countered this by changing to 72 spokes on the Mark I's optional wire wheels in place of the earlier 60-spoke pattern. Wire wheels were always preferred on the racing saloons to the standard steel wheels because they allowed better brake cooling.

The 3.4-litre Mark I saloons were also used with considerable success in rallying during the late 1950s, when the farming Morley twins, Don and Erle, had the most success. They won the Tulip international rally during a pre-harvest holiday! Bueb took over as the Equipe Endeavour team leader in circuit racing when Sopwith retired from competition driving in 1959, and Roy Salvadori starred in the Coombs car. Many other private owners acquired 3.4-litre Mark I saloons including, notably, Protheroe and Tommy Dickson. The 2.4-litre Mark I made some appearances in

competition, B.R. Waddilove winning his class in one in the 1958 RAC Rally. On the odd occasion, Peter Blond also beat Doug Uren's Ford Zephyr (which normally shared the honours in the medium-sized class up to 2.7 litres with Jack Sears in the ex-Wharton Austin).

### The Mark 2 saloons

Although the Mark 1 was a great success, selling four times as many as the larger Jaguar saloons, Lyons was not content. He knew it could be improved. Happily, virtually every aspect that had been criticized received attention in a new Mark 2 Jaguar saloon range introduced in October 1959. These cars were to rank among the best-loved Jaguars ever made, and they are still regarded as ultimate classics. The changes that were most readily apparent were in appearance. The windows were made larger, mainly by using slender roof supports now that it had become evident that those on the Mark 1 were thicker than necessary. The rear axle was also made much wider to remove the crab-tracked appearance, with the result that the new car's stability margin was greater. There were other detail changes including a redesigned interior that was not only more modern, but retained the traditional Jaguar image.

The Mark 2's performance was also made even more impressive by

*The 420G was one of the biggest yet most graceful cars on the road, with a truly luxurious interior, incorporating such items as occasional tables that were ideal for picnics. Provided by Graig Hinton.*

three new engine options, all using the B type cylinder head. The power of the 2.4-litre was increased to 120 bhp; that of the 3.4-litre to 210 bhp, and the Mark IX saloon's 3.8-litre engine was fitted to a new top-of-the-range model. This 220 bhp unit gave the Mark 2 a maximum speed of 201 km/h (125 mph) with a 0–60 mph acceleration figure of 8.5 seconds. The ultimate 265 bhp triple-carburettor straight-port cylinder head version of the 3.8-litre unit, as fitted to the XK150S sports car, was not used in the 3.8-litre Mark 2 because extensive changes would have been necessary to the engine bay to accommodate the extra carburettor. One of the reasons for using the 3.8-litre unit was that it produced far more torque than the smaller engines, which worked better with the automatic transmission now available as an option throughout the range. The limited-slip differential was fitted as standard to the 3.8-litre Mark 2 because the extra power and torque made it easy to wag the tail of the car when using full throttle from a standstill. Power-assisted steering, as used on the Mark IX saloon, was also offered as an option on the Mark 2, although only from October 1960 for the British market. This steering came in for criticism from some European customers who considered it too light, but the Americans for whom it was intended were well pleased: they were accustomed to ultra-light steering on their home-produced cars. Because of the Americans' apparent lack of interest in economy cars at that time, only the 3.8-litre Mark 2 was exported to the United States. It immediately established a reputation for being an exclusive, ultra-high-performance, medium-priced sports saloon, and as such was usually fitted with all the options: nearly all export Mark 2 Jaguars had wire wheels and whitewall tyres, for instance.

## Mark 2s in racing and rallying

The Mark 2 became an even more assured winner in saloon car races, now the 3.8-litre engine was available. It made its début in that form in Baillie's hands at Aintree in May 1960, but Salvadori won most races that year with a Coombs car. Moss and Sears were also notable performers in the Equipe Endeavour Mark 2s, but Lotus constructor Colin Chapman beat everyone during a guest appearance in the Coombs car at Silverstone in 1960!

More rallies were being changed to off-road courses, which did not suit the heavy Jaguar saloons, so the factory concentrated its support on the Tour de France. It was to be the start of four years of Jaguar dominance by the French team of Consten and Jack Renel, with some competition from Baillie and Peter Jopp. Jaguars were equally well suited to the fast roads of the Alpine Rally, in which the Appleyards had excelled a few years earlier; José Behra and René Benaud won the touring car category of this event in 1960 from Bobby Parkes and Geoff Howarth in another 3.8-litre Mark 2.

Circuit racing in 1961 became even more competitive with the advent of another top-line team of 3.8-litre Mark 2s entered by Peter Berry and driven by Bruce McLaren, Dennis Taylor and, sometimes, John Surtees. They provided stiff opposition for the established leaders, Salvadori in the Coombs car, and Mike Parkes and Graham Hill in Equipe Endeavour entries. The chief privateers at the time were Baillie, Bill Aston, Albert Powell and Vic Parness. However, the Jaguars were nearly beaten, for the first time, in the Silverstone Production Car Race by Dan Gurney's Chevrolet Impala, which used the power of its huge V8 engine to take the lead, until it lost a wheel. Hill won from Parkes with McLaren third. In Australia, Bob Jane for years raced a much-modified Mark 2 saloon, with its engine capacity increased to as much as 4.2 litres.

Hill joined Salvadori in the Coombs team in 1962, and Sears and Parkes represented the Equipe Endeavour. David Hobbs, Peter Woodroffe, Chris McLaren and Peter Dodd led the private entries; but Hill or Salvadori won most races. However, the threat of future trouble was reinforced by a victory over Salvadori by Charles Kelsey in a Chevrolet Chevvy 2 at Brands Hatch in May. The 3.8-litre Mark 2s were also quite successful in long-distance saloon car races providing that their tyre consumption could be kept under control. In 1962 Mike Parkes and Jimmy Blumer won *The Motor* Six-Hour race with their Equipe Endeavour car from the Germans Peter Lindner and Peter Nöcker in a similar machine. Lindner and Nöcker dominated European touring car races in 1962 and 1963 with a works-prepared 3.8-litre Mark 2, which they raced in addition to their lightweight E type. Their chief opposition came from a formidable team of Mercedes 300SE saloons, but even so they were not able to stop Peter Nöcker from winning the first European Touring Car Championship in 1963.

Jaguar started the 1963 season successfully with Lumsden, Peter Sargent, John Bekaert, Geoff Duke and Andrew Hedges using a standard 3.8-litre Mark 2 to break four international records by driving 16,093 km (10,000 miles) at 170.6 km/h (106 mph). In circuit racing Salvadori, with a 3.8-litre Mark 2 entered by magazine magnate Tommy Atkins, and Hill, in a Coombs car, continued to battle until they ran into really stiff opposition from Sears in a 7-litre Ford Galaxie. Baillie soon bought another Galaxie and the fight was on, with the enormous American cars winning in the dry

*ABOVE RIGHT The Jaguar 420 saloon, and its Daimler Sovereign equivalent were, in effect, compact versions of the 420G. This magnificent concours-winning 420, with optional wire wheels and sunroof, was provided by Gerry Margrave.*

*RIGHT INSET The 420 was based closely on the S type Jaguar saloon which used the 3.4- and 3.8-litre engines rather than the 4.2 unit. This example, provided by Philip Docker, has the optional Sundym tinted glass and wire wheels.*

and the nimbler British cars triumphant in the wet. One of the last great victories for the Mark 2 was when Salvadori and Denny Hulme won the Brands Hatch Six-Hour race at the end of 1963. That year Consten won the Tour de France for the fourth time despite a determined effort by the Galaxies and Ford's new Lotus Cortina, which was to take over the leadership of touring car races in 1964.

## The Mark X saloon

Lyons had kept abreast of technical trends by introducing a new large saloon to replace the ageing Mark IX. This was the Mark X of 1961, the first of a new generation of Jaguar saloons. In some respects it was similar to the E type sports car in that it used a wider version of the new independent rear suspension, with front suspension along the lines established by the smaller saloons. The rear suspension not only improved the car's handling but gave the rear-seat passengers a much better ride. The Mark X, which used the same 265 bhp engine as the E type, with the Mark IX's transmission options, was one of the widest cars ever made in Britain. It was also long and low, but the significant dimension was its width of 1930 mm (6 ft 4 in). Not only was the Mark X's body very large, but it was also exceptionally strong, being based on two massive sills—like the E type—with the steel floor to connect them. But, unlike the E type, the front wings and engine bay were part of the structure, as on the contemporary Mark 2 saloon. The interior was similar to the Mark 2, except that it was on a much bigger scale, making the Mark X a full six-seater. Its rear end was also redesigned to make the luggage boot (trunk) extremely large, following the example of the Mark IX—and particularly to please the American market. Unusually wide new wheels of only 14 inches diameter were used to fit in with its modern new appearance.

Because of the power of the E type engine, the Mark X was still capable of nearly 193 km/h (120 mph) despite its great weight of 1880 kg (4144 lb). Extensive use was made of rubber mountings to keep down the road noise created by this futuristic-looking new saloon. The appearance was thoroughly modern with new slim-line bumpers (as used on the XKSS design) and a four-headlamp system. The engine bay and bonnet were made as wide as possible, giving rise to speculation that the Mark X might be intended for use with the new V12 engine that Jaguar was developing at the time. As it happened, the new power unit underwent part of its testing in a Mark X saloon before it was introduced in the E type sports car in 1971. The Mark X sold reasonably well, but it was not an outstanding sales success, partly because the Mark 2 was in such demand and partly because it seemed too big for European roads.

## The Daimler acquisition

At the same time as the Mark X was being introduced in October 1961, the other end of the saloon car range was under consideration. Jaguar had bought Daimler in 1960 primarily to expand production facilities, but in the process the company had found itself with two excellent V8 engines. The larger of these, a 4½-litre, powered Daimler Majestic saloons and could have been used in the Mark X Jaguar, but it seemed likely to endow that car with such a high performance that the other Jaguar saloons would have suffered by comparison. In addition, one of the ways in which Jaguar kept down costs was by virtual standardization of items such as power units. So the 4½-litre V8 did not find its way into the Mark X. But the smaller, 2½-litre Daimler V8 gave such an improvement in the performance of the 2.4-litre Mark 2 saloon that it was put into production, because that was one car which could do with some extra urge. It was quite a simple conversion: the single-cam V8 engine (with a bore and stroke of 76.2 mm × 69.85 mm and capacity of 2548 cc) fitted into the Mark 2 with little modification. It was notably smoother than the 2.4-litre XK engine and lighter, which meant that the car handled better and the steering – which had been criticized for its heaviness—was lighter. In addition, the Daimler engine produced 20 bhp more power and significantly more torque, which gave the Daimler 2½-litre V8 saloon (as it was called) a performance roughly midway between the 2.4-litre Mark 2 Jaguar and the 3.4-litre. A new radiator grille, fluted in the traditional Daimler style, was fitted with different badges, and automatic transmission was standard, when the new car was introduced as an upmarket version of the 2.4-litre Mark 2 in November 1962.

## The S type saloon

There was a considerable demand for a more luxurious version of the compact saloon, and Lyons decided to combine the major improvements of the Mark X with the established features of the Mark 2, once the Daimler had been launched. The result was the Jaguar S type saloon

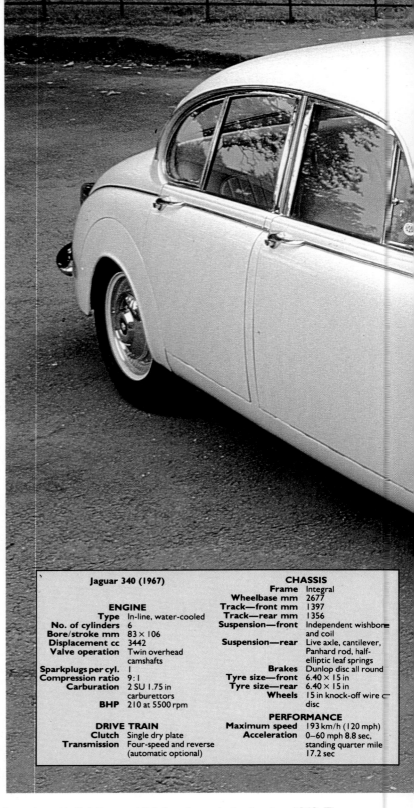

| Jaguar 340 (1967) | | |
|---|---|---|
| **ENGINE** | | |
| Type | In-line, water-cooled | |
| No. of cylinders | 6 | |
| Bore/stroke mm | 83 × 106 | |
| Displacement cc | 3442 | |
| Valve operation | Twin overhead camshafts | |
| Sparkplugs per cyl. | 1 | |
| Compression ratio | 9:1 | |
| Carburation | 2 SU 1.75 in carburettors | |
| BHP | 210 at 5500 rpm | |
| **DRIVE TRAIN** | | |
| Clutch | Single dry plate | |
| Transmission | Four-speed and reverse (automatic optional) | |
| **CHASSIS** | | |
| Frame | Integral | |
| Wheelbase mm | 2677 | |
| Track—front mm | 1397 | |
| Track—rear mm | 1356 | |
| Suspension—front | Independent wishbone and coil | |
| Suspension—rear | Live axle, cantilever, Panhard rod, half-elliptic leaf springs | |
| Brakes | Dunlop disc all round | |
| Tyre size—front | 6.40 × 15 in | |
| Tyre size—rear | 6.40 × 15 in | |
| Wheels | 15 in knock-off wire or disc | |
| **PERFORMANCE** | | |
| Maximum speed | 193 km/h (120 mph) | |
| Acceleration | 0–60 mph 8.8 sec, standing quarter mile 17.2 sec | |

introduced in 3.4-litre and 3.8-litre forms in September 1963. These cars were similar to the Mark 2 in most dimensions and running gear, except that they had the new independent rear suspension—in narrower form than on the Mark X—and extended rear bodywork, along the same lines as the big saloon, to give more room for luggage. The roofline was also changed slightly to increase headroom and the interior made plushier, like the Mark X and the new Daimler. The frontal aspect was tidied up and Mark X-style slim bumpers fitted. These new models were a great success (the Mark 2 continued virtually unchanged), but they were not used in competition because they were heavier. Soon after their introduction, the manual versions received a new all-synchromesh gearbox to replace the rather 'agricultural' unit that had served Jaguars so well since the XK120. The Mark 2 saloon eventually received this gearbox when sufficient supplies were available.

In the meantime, the Mark X was improved by fitting the 4.2-litre version of the XK engine—as used in the E type sports car—from October 1964. The reason for this change was that the extra torque of the 4.2-litre unit made the Mark X much smoother to operate and gave it better acceleration to keep pace with the latest developments in its American competitors.

## The 420 saloon and Daimler Sovereign

Lyons's next step was to ring the changes once again by fitting the 4.2-litre XK engine in twin-carburettor form into the S type saloon to produce the Jaguar 420—which was an immediate success as a truly luxurious compact saloon. This model, introduced in August 1966, also had its frontal aspect redesigned along the lines of the Mark X with a four-headlamp lighting system, but retained the original Mark 2 narrow bonnet opening to save extensive retooling. A Daimler version with the same engine and running gear, but with a fluted radiator grille and different badges, was introduced at the same time with the model name Sovereign. The Mark X also received a new radiator grille and a little extra chrome—and a new name, the 420G (for Grand)—to please its American distributors.

## The 240, 340 and Daimler V8 250

Next in line for revisions were the Mark 2 saloons and the small Daimler V8. Items such as leather upholstery were made optional extras to keep the price down and the 3.8-litre version was discontinued now that the 420 was in production (although the 3.8-litre S type was still listed). The expensive old Mark VII-style bumpers were replaced with slim-line versions like those on the other Jaguar and Daimler saloons. The new

*This is the 340 saloon which was similar to the earlier Mark 2, using the slim-line bumpers that were gradually introduced throughout the range from 1961. It finished its production run as Sir William Lyons had originally intended, as a compact economy model supporting the larger Jaguars. Provided by P. Chaplain.*

models, introduced in September 1967, were called the Jaguar 240 (with the 2.4-litre engine); the 340 (with the 3.4-litre engine); and the Daimler V8 250 (with the Daimler V8 engine).

All these cars were to be replaced from October 1968 by a brilliant new saloon, the Jaguar XJ6. But there was one final combination of their floorpans, bodywork, engines and transmission that is still in production today: the Daimler Limousine, introduced in June 1967 to replace British Leyland's Austin Princess, the 4½-litre Daimler Majestic Major limousine, and the occasional Jaguar Mark X or 420G with limousine fittings that had been produced in the 1960s. This enormous car, which used an extended version of the 420G floorpan with the 420G's running gear, was no less than 5740 mm (18 ft 10 in) long and a full seven-seater. As such, with bodywork designed by the British Leyland subsidiary, Vanden Plas, it sells for less than a quarter of the price of a Rolls-Royce.

# The best car in the world

The XJ6, which was to take over from Jaguar's rather confusing range of saloons in 1968, was one of the most significant cars made. It set new standards in handling, comfort and silence without losing any of the company's established attributes, such as performance and value for money. No wonder a *CAR* magazine panel voted it Car of the Year in 1968 and later, in 12-cylinder form with Daimler livery, the Best Car in the World. Although it was a big car, slightly longer (32 mm; 1¼ in), wider (76 mm; 3 in) and lower in overall height (38 mm; 1½ in) than the 420 from which it inherited most of its running gear, it was in fact based on the 420G. Its proportions were midway between those of the 420 and 420G and, as such, it was one of the best-looking Jaguars. The body followed the 420G's massive form of construction with a wide engine bay and bonnet opening to accommodate the V12 engine, which was still under development during the 1960s.

The new XJ6 (6 for six cylinders) was therefore introduced in October 1968 with either the 4.2-litre engine and transmission options previously available on the 420, or a new economy 2.8-litre version of the XK unit. This was based on the earlier 2.4-litre engine with a bore of 83.1 mm and stroke of 86.1 mm, giving a capacity of 2790 cc. This unit could be revved faster than the earlier XK engines because of its nearly square dimensions and, for a maximum power of 180 bhp, was fitted with the same straight-port cylinder head and SU carburettors as the 4.2-litre. This was enough to propel this relatively heavy new car to 190 km/h (118 mph) with a 0–60 mph acceleration time of around 11 seconds. Capable of 204 km/h (127 mph), the 4.2-litre XJ6 was slightly faster than the 420 because of its superior aerodynamics and could achieve 0–60 mph in 9 seconds.

The old team from Browns Lane showed that it had lost none of its touch with the XJ6. The lines were unmistakably those of Lyons, so much so that the name Jaguar appeared nowhere on the body because everyone knew it was the best of the 'Big Cats'! The engineering was the responsibility of Heynes. It was superb, particularly in the suspension, which varied in detail from that of the 420 and made the XJ6 one of the quietest saloons in the world, and probably the best-handling. The V12 engine that was to transform its performance from 1972 was developed by a team that included Hassan, who had returned to the fold when Jaguar took over the engine-builders Coventry-Climax in 1963, and Harry Mundy, who rejoined Chief Engine Designer Claude Baily as Chief Engine Development Engineer following a spell as technical editor of *Autocar* magazine. The team was further reinforced by Bob Knight who, as Chief Chassis Development Engineer, had been responsible for the refinement of every postwar Jaguar.

The designers were so successful in their efforts to keep down the road noise on the XJ6—mainly by the use of a sophisticated combination of rubber mountings—that they were able to use specially designed, very wide, radial-ply tyres from the start. These tyres, made by Dunlop, contributed enormously to the roadholding, but like all radial-ply tyres were inherently more noisy than the earlier cross-plies. The design was so successfully adapted that Jaguar led Rolls-Royce by four years, as the Crewe firm was not able to fit radial-ply tyres until 1972, when it had redeveloped its suspension. As a result, in terms of roadholding and handling, the Rolls-Royce Silver Shadow, which cost four times as much as an XJ6, was simply not in the same league as the Jaguar for this period. No wonder the XJ6 was an immediate success and had long waiting lists from the moment it was introduced. The Daimler Sovereign continued in production for a year until a Daimler version of the XJ6, also called the Sovereign, was launched; it bore the same model name and was distinguished only by a different radiator grille and badges. Daimler Sovereigns, however, sold for a higher price than the equivalent Jaguars and usually had more options fitted, such as electric windows. Production of the earlier Jaguar saloons was eventually terminated when the 420G ended in July 1970, so that as much space as possible could be devoted to XJ6 lines. Around 650 XJ6s were built every week; of these 100 went to the United States—only in Jaguar form as it was not considered worth the expense and complication of qualifying the Daimler version to be sold there. In fact 56 per cent of the total production was exported. During this period, from 1968 to 1972, extensive work was needed to meet US emission regulations and the introduction of the V12 engine had to be delayed several times until it was eventually fitted to the XJ in July 1972.

### The XJ12

The XJ12 was an astounding car: a full five-seater saloon capable of 233 km/h (145 mph) and a 0–60 mph time of only 7.4 seconds: faster than the majority of Grand Touring cars offering inferior accommodation and handling, and often costing three times as much. The only disadvantage was that the XJ12 used fuel at around 23.54 litres/100 km (12 mpg), which was not considered excessive for such a car at that time. There was an immediate demand for the XJ12 everywhere, even in countries where taxation and insurance were based on engine size. It proved the theory

*PREVIOUS PAGES Jaguar powered its way into the 1980s with the XJ12 high-efficiency model using new cylinder heads to improve fuel consumption—a point criticized on previous models, following the oil crises of 1973 and 1974. The results have improved the original consumption by as much as 40 per cent. Provided by Jaguar Cars Ltd.*

*RIGHT The XJ6 became a best-seller as soon as it was introduced in 1968; this 4.2-litre example was the personal transport of Sir William Lyons until his retirement in 1972. Provided by Jaguar Cars Ltd.*

*BELOW The XJ6 is so different from the average American automobile that it puts its owner in an exclusive category symbolizing good taste. This is a Californian-specification Series Two car provided by Ed Harrell.*

| Jaguar XJ6 4.2-litre Series One (1968) | |
|---|---|
| **ENGINE** | |
| Type | In-line, water-cooled |
| No. of cylinders | 6 |
| Bore/stroke mm | 92 × 106 |
| Displacement cc | 4235 |
| Valve operation | Twin overhead camshafts |
| Sparkplugs per cyl. | 1 |
| Compression ratio | 9 : 1 |
| Carburation | 2 SU 2 in carburettors |
| BHP | 245 at 5500 rpm |
| **DRIVE TRAIN** | |
| Clutch | Single dry plate |
| Transmission | Four-speed and reverse (automatic optional) |
| **CHASSIS** | |
| Frame | Integral |
| Wheelbase mm | 2762 |
| Track—front mm | 1473 |
| Track—rear mm | 1486 |
| Suspension—front | Independent wishbone and coil |
| Suspension—rear | Independent wishbone and coil, radius arms |
| Brakes | Girling disc all round |
| Tyre size—front | E70VR-15 |
| Tyre size—rear | E70VR-15 |
| Wheels | 15 in × 6K disc |
| **PERFORMANCE** | |
| Maximum speed | 204 km/h (127 mph) |
| Acceleration | 0–60 mph 8.8 sec, standing quarter mile 16.5 sec |

that if such potential customers could afford to tax an XJ12 they could manage to pay for the fuel; a view that was reinforced by the relatively small demand for the 2.8-litre, whose capacity had been aimed at taking maximum advantage of European tax laws. Lyons had always considered it wise to market an economical Jaguar, but at that time the majority went for those with the higher performance.

The XJ12 was available only with automatic transmission because there was no suitable overdrive that could cope with the engine's massive torque; but there was so much power and torque available in any case that the extra acceleration that manual transmission would have given was not needed. Apart from the engine, transmission and cooling system, there was little difference between the XJ6 and the XJ12: just more efficient ventilated front brake discs, higher speed rated tyres, and stiffer front springs to cope with the extra weight of the engine (308 kg; 680 lb against 272 kg; 600 lb). The engine bay was packed full, however, and the battery had to be fitted with its own fan to keep it cool! A Daimler Double Six version of the XJ12 was also introduced in 1972, along the lines of the Daimler Sovereign. Both the Daimler and Jaguar models had slightly different trim to their six-cylinder equivalents.

The 12-cylinder engine was not the only variant on the XJ theme that was introduced in 1972. A hurried decision was taken to 'stretch' the bodyshell by 102 mm (4 in) when Jaguar's chief rival, Mercedes-Benz, launched a new longer-wheelbase series. The idea, which was particularly successful on both marques, was to give back-seat passengers more legroom. Jaguar did it by inserting the extra length entirely in the rear compartment, behind the front door line. The weight penalty was only an extra 77 kg (170 lb) on an already hefty 1588 kg (3500 lb). Performance

was hardly altered, with an acceleration time to 60 mph of only half a second more. These new models, which became available throughout the range, carried an L suffix to denote the long wheelbase.

By that time, demand for the 2.8-litre XJs had fallen off to such an extent that this model was terminated in April 1973. A relatively ill-fated car, it was beset by piston problems during its early life and, in terms of performance, it paled in comparison with the larger-engined XJs. Only its superior fuel consumption (about 12.84 litres/100 km or 22 mpg against 17.66 litres/100 km or 16 mpg for the 4.2-litre XJ) and slightly lower price could be offered as advantages.

**The Series Two XJs**
American crash regulations were becoming more demanding every year, and these led to the introduction of a Series Two version of the XJ range in September 1973 that was carried over to the Daimlers in the interests of standardization. The main differences between the earlier cars and the Series Two models were in the outward appearance and in the interior. A new front bumper was fitted 406 mm (16 in) from the ground to comply with laws that decreed that fender heights should be standardized. However laudable the aim, this was really a waste of time and money for the car manufacturers, because in a crash the front of the car tended to be depressed by braking and the tail raised, so that the new bumpers missed each other anyway! Nevertheless, Jaguar managed to change the frontal appearance of its cars without making them unattractive, which was more than could be said for many manufacturers, whose efforts resulted in some extraordinary-looking machines. The interior was completely revised, making it more modern, with all the instruments grouped in front

of the driver, but it retained much of the old Jaguar 'walnut-and-leather' feeling. These changes were dictated not so much by a desire to modernize the interior as to meet the new safety regulations, which were far more realistic inside than outside the car.

The company used the opportunity afforded by these compulsory changes to redesign the Jaguar heating unit, which had been criticized for many years in one form or another. This was the first really modern heating/air conditioning unit to be fitted as standard to a Jaguar or Daimler, although air conditioning had long been available as an optional extra. The changes under the car's skin, such as the necessity to use a new bulkhead to accommodate the revised heating system, were achieved without losing any of the XJ's attributes, particularly its extreme silence of operation.

### The XJC

The Series Two models were introduced at the 1973 Frankfurt Motor Show alongside yet another variant on the XJ theme: a two-door coupé. This model, which carried the suffix C (for coupé), was especially significant in that it represented Sir William Lyons's last project before his retirement from active design in 1972. The XJC used the short-wheelbase floorpan with larger front doors and a slightly different roofline, but was otherwise substantially the same as the four-door saloons. However, there were considerable problems with sealing and raising and lowering the small rear windows, so the coupés did not go into production until early in 1975. Lyons had insisted that the front and rear windows met in a pillarless construction, which was very elegant, but posed many problems for the development engineers who had to keep down the wind noise on these fast cars! When they were eventually introduced, the option became available throughout the range, except on a Vanden Plas version of the Daimler, which was made in small quantities from 1973 to a higher standard of finish and trim than the Double Six. The coupés also remained in relatively restricted production because, by the time they had been introduced, the short-wheelbase floorpan had been dropped— everybody wanted a long-wheelbase XJ!

### The oil crisis and the economy models

Production of XJ6s carried on at the established high level as the world energy crisis during the winter of 1973 and 1974 hit sales of the XJ12. The effects of this crisis on cars such as the Jaguars and Daimlers with their high fuel consumptions led to a considerable number of changes in the range from April 1975. A 3.4-litre economy version of the XJ was introduced, using another version of the XK unit with the 'old' 3.4-litre bore and stroke measurements of 83 mm × 106 mm, in a new cylinder block designed to use the same tooling as the 4.2-litre. Fitting this engine improved fuel consumption to around 14.12 litres/100 km (20 mpg) on manual versions. The other noticeable effect of installing the new engine

was on the acceleration, which was reduced to 9.5 seconds for 0–60 mph. This proved acceptable to the customers who ordered the new 3.4-litre as an economy car, and as such it was available only in four-door saloon form, with cheaper trim as standard, or the normal trim as an option at extra cost. At the same time, an economy version of the Vanden Plas saloon with the 4.2-litre XK engine was introduced.

### The XJ-S

The range was also extended further by the introduction in April 1975 of a new Grand Touring version of the XJ, the XJ-S which had been under development since 1968. This two-plus-two seater fixed-head coupé was also meant to replace the E type sports car, which became defunct at the same time. When the design was under way in the late 1960s, it appeared that the Americans would legislate against open-topped cars in the interests of safety in roll-over accidents. However, such dramatic dictates were seen to be an infringement of the liberty of the people who wanted to buy these cars, but not before most manufacturers had stopped making open-top models. Unfortunately, this decision also came too late for Jaguar, who had decided that the XJ-S would have to be a fixed-head coupé and had designed the superstructure accordingly. This new body structure was mounted on an XJ floorpan, with its wheelbase shortened to 2590 mm (102 in), against the earlier 2764 mm (108.8 in) by moving the rear suspension forward and reducing the size of the rear-seat pan. The front bulkhead and engine-bay sides were modified to take the outer body and the screen pillars were made as strong as possible. Massive 8 km/h (5 mph) impact-absorbing bumpers were built in front and rear in a similar manner to those on the Porsches, the chief competitors in the GT field. The XJ-S's fuel tank was also moved forward to the front of the luggage compartment to protect it from possible impact (the extreme rear mounting of the E type sports car's tank was one of the reasons why it would not have met the 1975 American impact regulations).

Jaguar's four-speed manual gearbox was offered as an option without overdrive for ultimate performance. With a weight of just over 100 kg (225 lb) less than an XJ12, the XJ-S was endowed with a formidable performance of up to 240 km/h (150 mph) with a 0–60 mph figure of 6.7 seconds. Despite some criticism that its lines lacked the flare associated with Lyons, the XJ-S sold well to an impoverished world.

### Jaguar's return to competition

Jaguar sales, however, could not be compared with the glory years of the late 1960s and early 1970s although it must be said they were not so badly hit as those of many competitors in the luxury car field. Consequently it was decided by Jaguar's parent firm, British Leyland, to return to international competition with a works team. The decision was taken in 1976, when the XJC was still in production, to use the coupé for an assault on the European Touring Car Championship, which had given one of

*OPPOSITE AND LEFT Sir William Lyons kept his first XJ6 for three years, and then turned to a Daimler Double Six Vanden Plas, the ultra-luxurious model, based closely on the Jaguar XJ12, that was to be awarded the title of The Best Car in the World by CAR magazine in 1977. Provided by Sir William Lyons.*

Jaguar's rivals, the German BMW firm, a large amount of publicity. This made sense at the time because the XJC more closely resembled the standard XJ saloons than the lighter XJ-S. With the relatively untapped power of the 12-cylinder engine, British Leyland realized that it had a potential world-beater. The British tuning firm of Broadspeed was therefore commissioned to prepare a team of XJCs for long-distance racing, following a great deal of success with smaller Broadspeed Triumph Dolomites in saloon car racing.

It took Broadspeed most of 1976 to prepare the XJCs, however, because of the complex problems associated with making such a heavy car raceworthy. Power was the least of the tuners' problems—they extracted the best part of 600 bhp from their bored-out 5.4-litre engines. The British motor industry supported the effort magnificently, producing special wheels, brakes and tyres. The Jaguars became the great British national team whose début was eagerly awaited in the Tourist Trophy race late in 1976.

Derek Bell and David Hobbs duelled for the lead with a BMW 3.2CSL, driven by Jean Xhenceval and Pierre Dieudonné, before they were sidelined with a broken half-shaft, which was blamed on a flat tyre. Sadly, repeated trouble with items that included half-shafts, and a long delay before regulations allowed dry-sump lubrication, continuously defeated the Jaguars. They hardly finished a race in 1977 despite thrilling the crowds with amazingly fast practice lap times that frequently gave them pole position.

## The XJ-S in American racing
At the same time, the American Group 44 developed the XJ-S for racing in SCCA events. This was to be a different tale as the lighter car, driven by Bob Tullius and Brian Fuerstenau, swept all before it in 1976 and 1977.

Part of the reason for the success of the XJ-S, as opposed to the failure of the XJC, was that the American races were shorter and the cars—under SCCA regulations—were far nearer to standard. The European championship rivals, such as BMW, were simply too highly developed for the Jaguars to become fully competitive so quickly. The Broadspeed programme cost a fortune and British Leyland could not allow it to go on any longer without reward.

Meanwhile, the production XJ range was the subject of continuing development. Fuel injection was introduced in May 1978 on US-specification cars with 4.2-litre engines to reduce exhaust emissions and cut fuel consumption, followed by a new five-speed gearbox for manual cars in October 1978. This was fitted to rationalize production with Rover models, which were also made by British Leyland.

## The Series Three XJs and the XJ-40 project
Lyons had envisaged a production run of seven years when the XJ was introduced. But such was its reception and continuing popularity

RIGHT *Tim Schenken in the dry-sump XJ racing coupé leads team-mate Andy Rouse's wet-sump car at the start of the 1977 Tourist Trophy race at Silverstone. Twice the normal crowds turned out to cheer them on, but bad luck and a lost wheel defeated the Big Cats. The racing coupés started from pole position in most of their races.*

BELOW *The two-door, pillarless XJ coupé was produced only in small numbers and as such has an exclusive appeal, particularly because it was the last Jaguar to have been styled by the master, Sir William Lyons. The car shown here, a 1976 4.2-litre example, has been fitted with additional chrome piping to emphasize its lines. Provided by Roy Harris.*

(a Daimler Double Six Vanden Plas was acclaimed in 1977 as the Best Car in the World by *CAR* magazine as a result of comparison with Rolls-Royce, Mercedes and Cadillac) that it remained substantially unaltered when a Series Three version was introduced in March 1979. The Series Three changes applied to the entire range except the XJ-S and the XJC (which had been dropped because it had become uneconomic to produce it in small volume). The main changes in the Series Three were a raised roofline to give more headroom, and bumpers along the lines of those on the XJ-S to meet US safety regulations. An electrically operated sunroof was fitted—the first as standard on a Jaguar since the Mark IX—and the trim improved. Fuel injection was standardized on the 4.2-litre engine as work continued on the cylinder heads to reduce fuel consumption. This work, instigated by Mundy, was based on revolutionary 'Fireball' principles discovered by the Swiss engineer, Michael May. May had worked for the German Porsche design team for a while after he had pioneered another historic invention: the aerodynamic wing first used on his private Porsche Spyder racing car in 1956, 12 years before such devices were adopted on Grand Prix cars and developed for production machines. Later this gifted engineer went freelance and first showed the benefits of his Fireball combustion chamber design—improved economy, emission control and performance—on a Volkswagen Passat in 1976.

His Fireball design was essentially a split-level combustion chamber which ensured rapid and complete burning of a very lean fuel mixture. Jaguar redeveloped the XJ12's cylinder heads under licence from Michael May for a dramatic improvement in fuel consumption and a slight increase in performance when used in conjunction with a higher rear axle ratio. The additional torque and power generated by the May heads enabled the Jaguars to overcome higher axle ratios without a drop in performance and take advantage of them for improved fuel consumption when cruising.

LEFT *The latest of a long line of Jaguars, the XJ-S HE coupé (inset) showing, top, its luxurious new interior and, below, its revised engine with May cylinder heads. Provided by Jaguar Cars Ltd.*

RIGHT *The XJ-S proved more competitive in America than the XJ coupés in Europe. Shown here is the Group 44 car in an SCCA event.*

| Jaguar XJ-S HE (1981) | |
|---|---|
| **ENGINE** | |
| Type | Vee, water-cooled |
| No. of cylinders | 12 |
| Bore/stroke mm | 90 × 70 |
| Displacement cc | 5343 |
| Valve operation | Single overhead camshaft |
| Sparkplugs per cyl. | 1 |
| Compression ratio | 12.5:1 |
| Induction | Fuel injection |
| BHP | 299 at 5500 rpm |
| **DRIVE TRAIN** | |
| Clutch | Torque converter |
| Transmission | Automatic |
| **CHASSIS** | |
| Frame | Integral |
| Wheelbase mm | 2591 |
| Track—front mm | 1488 |
| Track—rear mm | 1473 |
| Suspension—front | Independent wishbone and coil |
| Suspension—rear | Independent wishbone and coil, radius arms |
| Brakes | Girling disc all round |
| Tyre size—front | 215/70 VR 15 |
| Tyre size—rear | 215/70 VR 15 |
| Wheels | 15 in × 6.5 K disc |
| **PERFORMANCE** | |
| Maximum speed | Approx 250 km/h (155 mph) |
| Acceleration | 0–60 mph 6.8 sec, standing quarter mile 14.5 sec |

After much experimentation, the new cylinder heads were introduced in July 1981 with a 2.8:1 rear axle ratio in place of a 3.07 on the 12-cylinder cars. The top speed was increased by about 8 km/h (5 mph) and the fuel consumption out of town improved to around 13 litres/100 km (22 mpg).

In addition, the XJ-S was revised in detail, in keeping with the Series Three saloons, with new bumpers, wheels and a much plushier interior. This new model was called the XJ-S HE (for high efficiency). The new cylinder heads, with attendant detail modifications to the engine, cost only £500,000—a remarkably small investment by the standards of 1981.

At the same time British Leyland was rationalizing its existing range of sporting cars by dropping the disappointing Triumph TR7 and TR8, which had been made in open form, and concentrating on design studies for a new open Jaguar. These were based on an open prototype on the XJ-S floorpan by the Italian coachbuilder Pininfarina, first shown in 1980. Pininfarina's rounded Jaguar XJ-S Spyder (the Italian name for a light open sports car) bore some resemblance to a Porsche 928 and there was a possibility that it would be put into production by 1983. Meanwhile, Jaguar had been given £75 million by British Leyland to develop a new saloon, code-named the XJ-40, with a target production date in 1984. It will have a new in-line six-cylinder engine of 2.8 or 3.2 litres with twin overhead camshafts and 24 valves in its high performance option. Later developments of the XJ-40 include a smaller XJ-80 and an F type tourer and coupé to replace the XJ-S which will closely resemble the E type of old. The chief aim of these projects is to produce more economical cars without losing any of Jaguar's long-established attributes of outstanding performance, quality and value for money. With so much at stake for such a great marque, the only object is to continue producing The Best Car in the World.

# Index

## Acknowledgements

The publishers wish to thank the following individuals and organizations for their permission to reproduce the photographs in this book:

*Autocar* 63 above; London Art Technical Drawings Ltd 36 above, 41 left, 77 inset; T.C. March 5 inset, 6-7, 19 inset; *Motor* 36 below, 41 right, 79; Rik Paul (special photography) 72.

All other photographs by Ian Dawson.

In addition, the publishers wish to thank Alan Hodge and his staff at Jaguar Cars Ltd, the Jaguar Drivers' Club and Graig Hinton of Classic Cars of Coventry Ltd. They would also like to thank the owners who kindly allowed their cars to be photographed.